PHILIP N͏͏
We͏ll
at
Castl͏   ͏ge
before ͏   ͏͏t Brunel
Universit͏,   ͏ualifying as a
chartered ͏ ͏veyor, he worked in
London and Hong Kong where he
and his second wife, Diane, lived for
thirty-three years. In 2005, Philip
began a new career in publishing and also set up his own business, offering editorial, design and photography services. He and
Diane returned to live in London in 2017, although they keep
a pied-à-terre in Hong Kong to escape the English winters.

To find out more about the author, visit philipnourse.com.

ONE LIFE TWO WORLDS

Philip Nourse

SilverWood

Published in 2021 by SilverWood Books

SilverWood Books Ltd
14 Small Street, Bristol, BS1 1DE, United Kingdom
www.silverwoodbooks.co.uk

ISBN 978-1-80042-087-8 (paperback)

British Library Cataloguing in Publication Data
A CIP catalogue record for this book is
available from the British Library

Page design and typesetting by SilverWood Books

One Life, Two Worlds

To Diane, my perfect wife, and my wonderful family

Why should I not publish my diary?
I have often seen reminiscences of people
I have never even heard of, and I fail to see –
because I do not happen to be a 'Somebody' –
why my diary should not be interesting.
My only regret is that I did not commence it
when I was a youth.

Charles Pooter
The Diary of a Nobody, 1892
George and Weedon Grossmith

Contents

Acknowledgements

First and foremost, I must thank my wife, Diane, not only for her forbearance during months of dedicated writing but also for her review of the manuscript and her helpful comments and suggestions.

I would also like to express enormous gratitude to Carol Cole, my professional book editor, who was introduced to me by a good friend in Hong Kong, Robert Wang, who published his own autobiography, *Walking the Tycoons' Rope*, in 2012. Carol guided me through the book, chapter by chapter, often encouraging me to open up as well as keeping a watchful eye on both syntax and grammar.

My thanks also go to the following, all of whom provided valuable input or reviewed sections of the manuscript: my brother, Christopher; my first wife, Elaine; my daughter, Sarah; Kate McQuillian, Archivist and Chapter Librarian at St George's Chapel, Windsor Castle; Maurice Kenwrick-Piercy, former chorister of St George's Chapel; Carol Dyer, author and editor; Richard Gocher, long-standing Hong Kong friend and business partner; John Chiu and Gordon Moffoot, former directors of Chesterton Petty Ltd; and Nicola Lisle, Writers Bureau tutor. Keith Macgregor, photographer and friend, also helped me by scanning a number of slides in 127-film format, dating from the 1960s, which my scanner could not manage.

And to all of those people I have omitted to mention, my apologies and grateful thanks.

Introduction

When the notion of writing my memoir began to take shape in the summer of 2019, my mind immediately focused on titles – what would I call the book? I toyed with the idea of *Ten Years Inside*, a title that came to mind many years ago when I first thought of writing a book about my life.

My editor was not enthusiastic. She felt it might give the wrong impression: readers might suppose that I had been detained at Her Majesty's pleasure. Her concern was understandable. This book is not about time spent 'inside'.

'Ten Years Inside' actually refers to the ten unforgettable years I spent living *inside* Windsor Castle during the late 1950s and the golden era of the 1960s.

Heeding my editor's advice, I struggled for months to come up with some more appropriate titles and finally settled on *One Life, Two Worlds* – encompassing my life in England and thirty-odd years spent in Hong Kong.

Staying in our winter home in Hong Kong at the beginning of 2020, we faced a challenge without parallel in the post-war years: a looming global pandemic. Accustomed to leading normal carefree lives, rubbing shoulders with family, friends and colleagues, we had to adjust our way of life in response to the coronavirus. Little did we know the world was about to undergo a transformation that would change all of our lives for the foreseeable future.

It was against this extraordinary backdrop that I was spurred into putting pen to paper. And so it was in Hong Kong that the greater part of this memoir was written: revisiting my life, digging up history and reliving memories from long ago. It has been an emotional journey, which I have enjoyed immensely.

Returning to our home in London in the summer of 2020, we were confronted with a second wave of the coronavirus – restrictions, isolation, soaring infection rates and innumerable deaths.

Since then, unable to escape the English winter, I have spent long hours fine-tuning my manuscript, sifting through thousands of photographs dating from the 1940s and culling ruthlessly.

Writing my memoir has been a source of real pleasure, giving me a sense of accomplishment that I have rarely experienced; taking me back to the time we lived in Windsor Castle, my working life in London and the fascinating years we spent in Hong Kong.

Poring over the manuscript again and again, I realize that my recollections are far from complete. I have surely missed many anecdotes and probably failed to describe my thoughts and feelings as fully as I would have liked. However, I sincerely hope there is enough material here to inspire and take the reader on a journey through a life so fully lived.

But let's go back to the beginning…

Philip Nourse
Barnes, London
December 2020

Chapter 1

The Early Years

1949-1957

My parents were born in 1922. My mother, Helen Jane MacDonald
Allison, was born in Glasgow and brought up in Scotland. She was
the youngest of five siblings, having two brothers and two sisters. I
regret that I know so little about my mother's family and upbringing,
other than that the family home was in Glasgow and they had a
cottage in Brodick on the Isle of Arran in the Firth of Clyde, where
they spent their summers. My father, John, was born and raised in
Shute, Devon, where my grandfather, whom I never knew, was the
vicar. My father was also the youngest member of his family and
also had two brothers and two sisters.

My father was educated at Sherborne School in Dorset and St
John's College, Cambridge, where he was a choral scholar and studied
for a bachelor's degree in music. He initially read natural sciences with
the intention of becoming a doctor but this course was abandoned
and he concentrated on music studies.

After two years at Cambridge and receiving a 'wartime degree', he volunteered for the navy and joined the Royal Naval Volunteer Reserve (RNVR) as a rating in 1942. He was earmarked early on as officer material and, after sea time and training, was promoted to sub-lieutenant RNVR the following year.

In the summer of 1943, my father was posted to HMS *Nimrod*, the Anti-Submarine School in Campbeltown on the Mull of Kintyre in Scotland. My mother had joined the Women's Royal Naval Service (WRNS) and was also based in Campbeltown. The Wrens, as this branch of the navy was generally known, was re-established in 1939 following its disbandment after the end of the First World War.

It was in Campbeltown that my father met Leading Wren Helen Allison, who was living in the Wrens' quarters. On 18th May 1945, my parents were married in St Margaret's Church in Newlands, Glasgow, following which they spent a few days' honeymoon in the North British Hotel (now The Balmoral) in Edinburgh and a week in Bude, Cornwall, with my father's family.

In 1946, following Father's release from the navy, my parents moved to Salisbury in Wiltshire, where my father taught at the Cathedral School. My brother, Christopher, was born in Salisbury in August of the same year.

After two years in Salisbury, my father was interviewed by the principal of Wells Theological College in Somerset and accepted as a married student. My parents moved to Wells in January 1948. Married students were expected to live in college lodgings and make arrangements for their families to be boarded elsewhere. So my mother and Christopher were installed in a flat on the third floor above a shop in the High Street, while my father lived in Vicars' Close next to the cathedral.

On 21st October 1949, I was born. The family moved into a bungalow on the Bath Road, now sadly surrounded by hundreds of other bungalows and houses, but in those days looking out across the fields towards the Mendips.

In December of that year, my father was ordained into the ministry in Winchester Cathedral and we moved to Bournemouth in Dorset at the suggestion of my godfather, Philip Sprent, who was Vicar of St Augustin's Church. My father's appointment was as curate.

This was not the happiest period of my father's career. My mother did not seem to be well much of the time and did not recover fully from my birth. What is now known as post-natal depression began to set in and the first of a long line of doctors and pills began to appear.

I believe that my parents' marriage was going through a difficult time – even at this early stage – but they survived and set off to Sussex, where my father was appointed as a teacher at Hurstpierpoint College. My brother, Christopher, would later go to school there.

Of course, I have no recollection of this time but we lived in a house called Rectory Cottage near the old rectory in the village of Hurstpierpoint. My father seemed to enjoy this time, teaching mainly in the Junior School.

My mother's ailments continued and she underwent two major abdominal operations, both of which it transpired were not necessary. She was in and out of hospital a good deal and my paternal grandmother came to stay and help. My parents also employed a girl to look after Christopher and me.

Although ordained, my father was not the chaplain at Hurstpierpoint College. After two years, the incumbent chaplain left and the headmaster asked if my father would like to take over the chaplaincy. However, there was no housing provided and, given the family circumstances, he reluctantly decided he could not take up the offer.

This position would undoubtedly have been an excellent opportunity. In the event, the Bishop of Guildford was a great help and, in the autumn of 1952, my father was appointed Priest-in-Charge of St Mark's, Peaslake in Surrey.

Aged three, my first memories are of Peaslake. We lived in a lovely parsonage in the country, where we stayed for five years. The house, built in the 1930s in mellow brick, had a double drawing room, a study, a dining room and a large kitchen. Upstairs, there were four bedrooms and a bathroom. There was a big garden with a large hut, apple trees and a swing. The sun came beating down across the lawn onto the French windows, with views looking west to Newlands Corner.

Outside the front door was a large drive where my father parked the family saloon, a rather grand black Vauxhall Velox with a six-cylinder engine and a top speed of seventy-four miles an hour. I can even remember the number plate: NPG 950. He also owned what he called a 'popper', a motorized bicycle – an early forerunner of today's electric bicycles – which I learned to ride when I was older.

Christopher and I had a lot of fun. We used to play in the garden and pick apples. I remember smoking lavender, which grew abundantly around the house, and mucking around with bits and pieces in the hut.

One hot summer night, we decided to sleep under canvas in the garden. I think my mother probably pleaded some ailment and sensibly decided to remain indoors. Unfortunately, there was a huge thunderstorm with heavy rain.

'Come on,' my father called, suddenly awakened by the storm in the middle of the night. 'Let's get inside.'

'Can't we stay in our tents, Daddy?' Christopher pleaded.

'No, it's too dangerous. Come on.' And we all had to make a very hasty retreat indoors where we faced Mother, who had come downstairs, a note of mockery in her voice.

I used to creep out of bed at night to check that my father and mother were downstairs in the drawing room – perhaps the precursor of an insecurity which endured for some years, apparently the result of my mother having been unwell and absent for significant periods of my early childhood. I was later to leave notes for my father saying

'KS' or 'Keep Safe', which I think continued until I went to boarding school at the age of eight. My father was very caring and kept these notes for years.

My parents employed a live-in girl called Phyllis to look after Christopher and me and to help generally. She was quite a character. There was a drama one day when I went missing. I have no idea why I went wandering off – a naughty prank, perhaps – but there was a huge sense of relief when I was discovered somewhere up the lane near the house. Phyllis married a local boy called John and my father conducted the marriage ceremony in Peaslake Church in 1955, with Christopher and me apparently dressed up in kilts as pages!

I started to have piano lessons at this time. I was taught by a Miss Cureton and another teacher too, Miss Lejeune. They were good teachers and gave me an excellent grounding in playing, which I would continue to do for many years to come.

'You must practise harder, Philip. You must practise your scales every day,' Miss Cureton would tell me regularly. I have never enjoyed practising scales but I did apply myself, which no doubt put me in good stead for the future.

Peaslake was a very high-powered parish socially, with all sorts of well-known artists and writers and wealthy stockbrokers. My parents were invited to innumerable cocktail parties and I was sometimes looked after by the Walkers, who lived in a large house and frequently offered me real hot chocolate – proper chocolate flakes melted in hot milk.

I attended a school called Cockers Hill, which Christopher had attended before me. I have few recollections other than learning to read and being picked up from school one afternoon by a friend of my parents in a Morris Minor and skidding down the hill on black ice.

Miss Moody, the headmistress, wrote in her report for the summer term, 1956:

Philip is proving a delightful child to have in the class. He works
hard and seems to enjoy doing this. He has a keen sense of humour.
*   If he continues to develop as he has begun, he should be up to*
the required standard or beyond when he leaves.

We all loved Teddy, a black furry dog given to my father when he lived in Salisbury. He roamed freely all over the village, which was quite normal in those days – no doubt siring a few puppies along the way – and getting into all sorts of dangerous scrapes. Sadly, one day he never returned. We waited for him to come home and bark outside as he did at night sometimes when he'd been out, but he never came. My father was heartbroken and made enquiries of the police, the RSPCA and Battersea Dogs Home. He was never found. There were some Polish farmworkers on a farm nearby who probably didn't like Teddy because he used to bark at them – and perhaps the sheep too. We believe that he may have been shot and buried, but we never knew.

A year after Teddy disappeared, my parents acquired another dog, a golden retriever called Marcus. He was a beautiful dog, if not the most intelligent, but was sadly given to the daughter of one of Father's colleagues sometime after we moved to Windsor Castle; partly because it was generally felt that a dog was not suitable in the cloisters, where we lived, and also because he really wasn't happy without long country walks. It was a difficult decision, but a sensible one, and he enjoyed life with his new owner.

The years following the Second World War were lean. Like so many others during this period, my parents needed to be prudent with money but, while there were no non-essential purchases, I do not recall us ever going without. In those days, very few women worked after they were married and did not contribute to the household income. As a priest, my father took home a modest stipend – I recall a figure of around £400 a year.

Rationing, introduced in January 1940 to ensure fair shares for all, continued after the end of the war. When the Queen came to the throne in 1952, sugar, butter, cheese, margarine, cooking fat, bacon, meat and tea were all still rationed. Food rationing did not actually finish until 1954. To buy most rationed items, purchasers had to present ration coupons to shopkeepers with whom they had registered. I remember shopping with my mother in the local stores. Meals at home were simple but adequate, often supplemented by vegetables grown in the garden.

Petrol rationing ended earlier, in 1950, but was reintroduced in January 1957 for five months during the Suez Crisis when Egypt and Syria blocked supplies.

There was no central heating in the average home and, although fridges were becoming more common, freezers were unheard of. If you were lucky enough to have a washing machine, it would be a twin-tub with a mangle on top. There were no supermarkets, so my mother would visit the local baker, the butcher, the greengrocer and the grocer one by one.

Most households had a vacuum cleaner and a cooker. Entertainment was provided by the wireless or gramophone, although more and more people were acquiring televisions. My first memory of a television set in our home – made of Bakelite – was in 1956. These, like telephones, were rented, not owned. All television programmes were in black and white and there were only two TV channels to watch: the BBC and the commercial channel.

After five years in Peaslake, it was time for my father to move on to a new position. It came about that a minor canonry at St George's Chapel, Windsor Castle, became vacant. My father went for an audition with the Dean and Chapter and was offered the post. The move to a town, to a house with no garden, was in complete contrast to the country life enjoyed in Peaslake but it was the beginning of a completely new chapter in my life.

Chapter 2

Windsor Castle

1957-1963

In February 1957, the family moved into No 10 The Cloisters, Windsor Castle; for me, ten formative years that would change my life. Christopher was ten and I was seven.

One of my first memories of No 10 was arriving at a rather grand mulberry-coloured front door with a black iron bell-pull with a notice beneath it saying: 'Please do not ring unless an answer is required.' This was a four-storey house, plus basement, and I suppose that residents of the house were reluctant to climb up and down innumerable stairs to answer an unnecessary call. In November 2019, Christopher and I revisited the house, where it appears the same bell-pull exists – but without the words underneath.

The atmosphere of the castle itself was, of course, unique. We entered under the Henry VIII Gateway, where uniformed soldiers stood sentinel with their rifles and bearskins. Police were present too; if they knew you, they would let you in. Today, security is much tighter. Then you passed through the Horseshoe Cloister, opposite the west end of St George's Chapel, with plane trees and beautiful buildings all around you. There was a feeling that you were in the Royal Palace. There were guards and police padding about all day and night. I don't believe we ever locked the doors while we lived there.

Numerous visitors poured through the castle and cloisters, visitors of all nationalities, who the residents felt were an intrusion into their privacy. My father told me that they used to look at our front door with the figures 'one nought' on it and he could hear people with confused ideas saying, 'Look, it's No 10', and he supposed that they thought the prime minister lived there.

No 10 is situated in the Canons' Cloister, which dates from the fourteenth century and forms part of the foundations of the College of St George. Construction work on the original buildings of the Canons' Cloister began in 1351 and was completed in 1355. It seems that the west end of the cloister was destroyed or damaged beyond repair in the 1640s, during the Civil War. It was rebuilt in the 1660s, following the restoration of the monarchy in 1660, as Nos 9 and 10 – now St George's House, founded in 1966.

The house was arranged on lower-ground, ground and three upper floors. The front door led into the main hall and the dining room, which had tall sash windows, high ceilings and wood-panelled walls. It faced west and overlooked what is now known as Denton's Commons. (Denton's Commons, the former common house for chantry priests and choristers, was built in 1519 and originally referred to the lower part of this area.) Besides the dining table, sideboard and chairs, there were two armchairs and a television. This room was the main focus of everyday living. The back door opened onto the Canons' Cloister. Immediately adjoining the back door was the chapel choristers' vestry, a room that I would come to know well.

Downstairs was the kitchen at lower-ground-floor level, a rather large old-fashioned kitchen with barred windows, the top half of which allowed a restricted view of the outside world. There was a rope-and-pulley dumb waiter, which fascinated Christopher and me, serving the dining room above. My parents did not enjoy this rather dark and inconvenient space and created a kitchenette next to the back door on the ground floor. This served our everyday needs, with a Belling cooker, fridge and sink.

My father told me the story – possibly apocryphal – of some visitors looking into the kitchen through the half window and, unable to resist the temptation, he seized the bars, screaming up at them, 'Help, help. Someone let me out. I've been locked down here for years.' They ran away, looking frightened. Such was my father's humour and dislike of the hundreds of visitors who passed our house every day. Two years after we arrived, Canon Bentley, who lived almost next door in No 8 The Cloisters, instigated the closure of Denton's Commons to visitors, egged on by my father, so that the residents could enjoy some privacy. This plan was indeed implemented, much to the relief of all.

Another amusing memory of our basement kitchen was when Christopher and I decided to play a very unfair prank on our daily, Mrs Watson.

'Mrs Watson, we've just cooked breakfast and thought you might enjoy a fried egg,' I said, offering her the tempting plate as she came towards the kitchen table.

'Oh, thank you, dears, how kind,' she said and tucked in with knife and fork, only to find that she was cutting into a plastic egg.

'You are wicked, you boys, I don't know.' Poor Mrs Watson, who did not have the best eyesight, was taken aback and laughed awkwardly. No doubt we sniggered but we should have been ashamed of ourselves.

Surrounding the basement kitchen were tunnels and caverns (ideal as a wine cellar but not used as such) in which Christopher and I played the 'Prince Game', when Christopher played the prince, dressed in grand clothes – a gold-coloured bedspread – with me as the servant (or pauper). There were probably swords involved but I forget exactly how the role play worked. We also played the 'Office Game', with Christopher as managing director and me as a mere assistant, of course. Today, this area is now the central kitchen for St George's House, providing food for a full house of delegates attending conferences.

On the first floor, immediately above the dining room and also looking down Denton's Commons to the Chapter Library and Marbeck Hall, with the King's Beasts* looking benignly down on the scene from the chapel parapet, was the drawing room, which was entered through arched double doors. This was a beautiful room with a pair of tall sash windows, an Adam fireplace and Regency-striped wallpaper. Outside the drawing room was a short passage leading to a small cloakroom. There was an oak chest where Christmas presents were sometimes hidden – and usually inspected by me before the big day!

My father's study was on the east side of the house, overlooking the Canons' Cloister. It was in this room that I built Meccano models with my father, including a working clock. After much experimentation, we found that it required a pendulum stretching from the first-floor window to the Canons' Cloister below to achieve any semblance of proper timekeeping. It was also here that I learned the golden rule of never putting anything in writing, after my father came across some schoolboy correspondence referring to 'Jessica Stephens in the nude'. I have remembered this valuable piece of advice to this day.

The six bedrooms were situated on the second and third floors, all served by one family bathroom. On the second floor, my parents

---

* *The original King's Beasts, which dated from the Tudor period, were removed in the seventeenth century and replaced with seventy-six new beasts between 1925 and 1928 during the reign of George V.*

occupied the largest bedroom; the equally large adjoining bedroom, with a connecting door, was occupied first by Christopher and later by me. I originally had the smallest bedroom. For some reason, we later switched bedrooms and Christopher moved into the smaller of our bedrooms – perhaps he felt it was more private.

On the top floor were three further bedrooms, the biggest of which was our playroom. Outside was a huge cupboard, which was full of our Dinkies, a Bayko building set, oak building blocks, train sets and all sorts of paraphernalia. The valuable Meccano set was kept in Father's study. We set up entire towns in this room, with Hornby trains (and larger-gauge trains too), Dinky vehicles and Bayko houses. We were very privileged children, having so much space and many toys. (Sadly, I never had a Scalextric set, first introduced in the late 1950s.)

The toys have all gone. The Dinkies were sold to our second helper, Susie Pomfrett, for a meagre £5 before she and her husband emigrated to Australia. I have no idea where the remaining toys ended up, except for a Hornby O Gauge, Type 40 black tank engine in British Railways livery that I gave my daughter, Sarah, many years ago. A recent visit to eBay indicated prices for these vintage models ranging from £40 up to £95. Many of our other toys – the Dinkies and Meccano set in particular – would command high prices today.

One day, Christopher and I decided to redecorate our playroom. After much discussion and agreement with our parents, it was decided that the walls should be painted primrose yellow, the woodwork dove grey. The paintbrushes and various other accessories, including a small blue bowl for mixing paint, were duly acquired and work commenced. We did a fine job. However, the 'little blue bowl', as it came to be known, which was coated with dove-grey paint, was never cleaned properly and the paint, of course, was ingrained for life. My father never forgot this – a reminder of our sloth and material waste, which haunted us for years. It became a family joke and he would occasionally remind me of the little blue bowl until the day he died.

There was a fire-escape door in our playroom with a key in a red glass-fronted box on each side. This 'secret' door led into the top floor of No 9 The Cloisters. Donald, a minor canon and colleague of my father, lived there. Donald was a strange character, gentle and quiet, hospitable and kind. He came to our house often for tea and lunch, and sometimes Christmas dinner. He was a bachelor and enjoyed the company of young men. He was a good friend of the family, taking Christopher and me on outings.

Donald was an aficionado of Gilbert and Sullivan, owning all the records of their Savoy operas and playing them frequently in his house. He took us to the Savoy Theatre in London to see the D'Oyly Carte Opera Company perform almost every opera that Gilbert and Sullivan had ever written – not once, but sometimes twice. At some stage, Christopher and I decided to be rather wicked, having tired of constant Gilbert and Sullivan. We would keep absolutely straight faces when we were supposed to laugh; and when it was supposed to be serious, we laughed. I suspect that Donald did notice because he would look round at us with enquiring and disapproving glances.

Donald became rather over-familiar and he would creep through the secret door, having opened the red key box on his side, and leave gifts or notes for us. Christopher and I hatched a plan. If we were away, we used to build a barricade on our side of the door, made of boxes, records, toys and anything else we could lay our hands on. If Donald entered our territory – as he did from time to time – the whole barricade would come crashing down; he had been 'caught'. He used to make a hasty retreat, leaving the wreckage untouched. The unwanted secret intrusions ceased.

The second bedroom on the third floor was a spare room, which was sparsely furnished and the only bedroom where we could accommodate visiting family and friends. My mother's sisters and in-laws were regular visitors, no doubt eager to catch a glimpse of everyday life in the royal castle. My father's sisters would also stay, and one of my three maternal great-aunts, who lived in the Scottish Highlands, made the long journey south on at least one occasion.

There was another tiny bedroom on this floor, which was let to an elusive character called Gerald Leet. He rarely appeared and one never knew exactly what he was or where he had been. He had rented this room before we arrived in No 10 in 1957, so we inherited him as a tenant.

Gerald died in 1998 and was described in his obituary in *The Independent* as an art master, a painter, a book collector and man of mystery.

> From humble beginnings, he worked his way into accommodation at Windsor Castle, Queen Elizabeth The Queen Mother having commissioned from him a series of portraits of her staff. He served as official war artist in New Delhi and taught at Eton. Nothing gave him greater pleasure than to compartmentalize his life and friends and to tantalize dealers with offers to sell books and paintings which often failed to materialize.
>
> In September 1946, Leet was appointed Assistant Drawing Master at Eton, where he worked under the legendary Wilfred Blunt, Art Master from 1938 to 1959. He remained at Eton until 1949, when he moved into Windsor Castle, working three days a week as a teacher at Brighton College of Art while executing a series of portraits for the Queen Mother. He specialized in portraits of the great and famous, claiming intimate friendship with the Mountbattens, Field Marshal Auchinleck and assorted Turkish princes and Greek princesses.

Leet had a brother who predeceased him, but no other family, depending for intermittent entertainment on a wide circle of friends, who recall him as a brilliant conversationalist and mimic but an inveterate name-dropper. He lived for many years in Brighton, in a modest flat crammed with *objets d'art*, rare books and fine paintings. In old age, he assumed the mantle of a sparkling and amusing elderly raconteur. Yet he remained a very private person.

Whether there was ever any great secret in need of suppression may be doubted. More likely, he enjoyed sub-terfuge for its own sake. He would suddenly appear in a local bookshop with some precious object that might or might not be for sale, and as suddenly disappear again for months. He seemed always to be putting people to some sort of test, and not many passed. Those few who did pass muster were richly rewarded.

In his late years, he suffered two strokes and finally moved into a Brighton nursing home, where he died after returning the previous day to his flat to retrieve some of his favourite paintings.

Gerald Mackenzie Leet, painter, teacher and collector: born London 1913; died Brighton 18 June 1998.

Courtesy: Michael De-la-Noy
The Independent, 25th June 1998

And a man of mystery he remained to us; full of charm on the rare occasions we met, an idiosyncratic figure. Christopher has a rather lovely oil painting of a kitchen scene, painted by Gerald Leet, and given to us for reasons unknown.

In 1964, we were advised by the Dean and Chapter that No 10, along with Donald Fehrenbach's adjoining house, was to be transformed into a conference centre and that we would need to move to another house in the cloisters – No 24.

There have been buildings on the site of No 24 – along with Nos 25 and 26 – since the late twelfth century. However, the history of these houses is complicated because they have not always used the same numbering system as they do now. The part of the building now known as No 24 is believed to have been built as an annex to the part known as No 25 in about 1720. The building was then known as No 12 until 1859 when the adjacent No 11 was found to be unfit for habitation. No 11 was demolished, additions and alterations were made to No 12 and it became Nos 24, 25 and 26.

My father was very close to the dean, Robin Woods, who undoubtedly made the planned move very much more palatable. After the initial shock, my parents warmed to the idea: a better house, infinitely more manageable and with proper central heating. However, there was a problem with the kitchen – once again, situated on the lower-ground floor – and my parents insisted, as a condition of moving, that a new kitchen be built as an extension to the dining room on the ground floor. This was agreed and in 1965 we finally moved into a very lovely four-bedroom house with a brand-new kitchen – with the bonus of a terrace on the roof of the kitchen. The drawing room was situated on the ground floor and the four bedrooms on the first and second floors, one of which, on the first floor, became my father's study, with direct access to the terrace.

There was an added bonus: the lower-ground floor, which had its own front door with direct access from Denton's Commons, comprised the former kitchen, two bedrooms and a bathroom. There was also a staircase leading up to the main house, where my mother would occasionally be caught listening to my telephone conversations with girlfriends. This was where Christopher and I resided – in almost complete privacy – with our own bedrooms and a 'studio' (the former kitchen), although Christopher was away at Edinburgh University during term time so I was often alone. It was in the studio that I pursued my hobbies of photography and painting. One of the paintings, an oil painting based on a Toulouse-Lautrec, which I finally framed fifty-three years after I completed it in 1966, now hangs in our study in Barnes. There is also another of my paintings, titled *Fidra* (an island off the North Berwick coast in Scotland), dated 1967, which now hangs in our drawing room.

I have many memories of No 24, both happy and sad. By and large, I relished life as a teenager. Christopher and I had good friends, with whom we had a great deal of fun, and I enjoyed falling in love – lots. And yet, growing up and discovering myself, I often felt a deep melancholy that I cannot easily explain. I remember, when I was younger, my mother once whispering to my father that I was a very emotional person. She was right and I was now going through a difficult age.

Following complete renovation and conversion, Nos 9 and 10 became St George's House. It was opened in 1966 by HRH The Duke of Edinburgh and the Dean of Windsor, Robin Woods, as 'a place where people of influence and responsibility in every area of society could come together to explore and communicate their views and analysis of contemporary issues'.

The Duke of Edinburgh believed that, as the house was hidden away within the castle walls, it was particularly suitable to attract people in positions of leadership within government, industry, commerce and the churches as a place for discreet discussions of mutual and national interest.

According to historian Robert Lacey, the Duke of Edinburgh liked Robin Woods' proposal for the conference centre and helped to raise the money needed to renovate and convert the houses. When it was opened on 23rd October 1966, the Duke of Edinburgh gave a forty-minute introduction speech and then moderated a debate. He continued to stay involved in his later years, even publishing a book in 1982 which features the philosophical lectures and speeches he's given there. Two more editions were subsequently published.

Today, St George's House is an elite institution, established over fifty years ago in the house where Christopher and I lived for the first eight years of our magical time in Windsor Castle.

For those of us who are familiar with the third series of Netflix's *The Crown*, the 1969 moon landing catapults Prince Philip, Duke of Edinburgh, into an existential crisis. He is inspired by the feat, but unimpressed with the American astronauts' reflection on what he sees as an extraordinary experience. In search of guidance, he turns to the dean and founds St George's House, an organization dedicated to the exploration of faith and philosophy.

As with many aspects of the British royal family's life, *The Crown* producers took some liberties with the details and strayed from reality. St George's House was established in 1966 – three years before the moon landing. *The Crown* star Tobias Menzies, who plays Philip, apparently said there was no evidence that his real-life counterpart became fascinated with the moon landing, but that the storyline allowed the programme to explore 'the more complicated feelings Philip might have about what he's done with his life'.

St George's Chapel is one of the finest examples of the Perpendicular style of Gothic architecture in England. The College of St George was founded by Edward III in 1348 as 'a College of Canons, Presbyters, Clerks and Knights…who in the same Chapel shall evermore wait upon the Lord's service'. The Most Noble Order of the Garter was founded at the same time.

The College now consists of 'the Chapel, St George's School, St George's House, the Military Knights of Windsor, the Chapter Library and Archives and the Choir'. St George's is a Royal Peculiar, meaning a church under the direct jurisdiction of the monarch and exempt from the jurisdiction of any diocese or bishop.

The chapel was built in two stages. The quire and its aisles were completed and roofed by 1483 and the nave by 1509. However, the chapel was not finally completed, including the stone fan vaulting, until 1528.

When we arrived in Windsor in February 1957, Christopher was already away at school but my schooling had not yet been arranged. I was auditioned for St George's, the choir school, and was accepted as a chorister. Since they could not take me immediately because there were no places available, I went to Upton School, a small school in St Leonard's Road, which some of the royals later attended.

I spent three terms at Upton School before joining St George's in January 1958. I started as a dayboy before becoming a chorister. As a chorister, I was required to be a boarder, the irony being that my parents lived a short walk away, next to the vestry where I would spend so much time changing for chapel services. At the time, the school had eighty boys: twenty choristers, the remainder 'supers' (short for supernumeraries). Now, of course, the school is co-educational, with over 300 pupils.

And so began an extraordinary chapter in my life: singing in one of the finest choirs in the country, before royalty and at major events. There was the splendour and panoply of the ceremonies, the majesty of the chapel itself, with the banners of the Knights of the Garter glowing above the stalls in the quire and some stalls carved with names of many generations of choristers, and of course the beautiful music which was such an integral part of my everyday life. I was indeed privileged, and I knew it.

When I first arrived at St George's, the organist and master of the choristers was Sir William Harris, familiarly known as Doc H by the choristers, lay clerks and pretty much everybody else as well.

Doc H was an outstanding musician and composer. He ensured that the choristers performed to their very best.

The routine of a chorister was demanding, with choir practices or sung services every day except Wednesday. We walked up many steps from the school to the Marbeck Hall (named after John Marbeck, the organist of St George's Chapel from about 1541) for choir practice at 8.15 am and 4.00 pm on Mondays, Tuesdays, Thursdays and Fridays. We were worked hard and, as a soloist, I was expected to perform at my peak. Passages were repeated over and over again until perfection was achieved.

After choir practice, we walked over to the vestry, next to No 10, where we changed into cassocks, surplices and Eton collars for mattins at 9.15 am and evensong at 5.00 pm. There were no sung services on Wednesdays or Saturday mornings. On Sundays, we sang three services: mattins at 10.45 am, Holy Communion an hour later and evensong at 5.00 pm. Today, the timetable of chapel services is different, although not significantly, and the choristers sing fewer services – presumably to lighten the burden of twelve services every week.

We were required to remain in residence, as boarders, over Christmas and Easter. This was difficult as the supers – non-choral pupils – all set off for the school holidays and were able to enjoy the celebrations with their families. The choristers went home after Christmas and Easter were over. Our holidays were, of course, a little shorter but this was the price we paid for the privilege of singing in St George's Chapel. Many boys enjoyed the stay-on: some relaxation of school rules, the Queen's Private Secretary taking us to the theatre and some well-heeled parents donating high-quality presents at Christmas – far nicer than many parents could afford.

I recall one amusing incident when the Queen attended a Sunday service. The dean, then Eric Hamilton, led her into the quire at the tail end of the procession of choir and clergy and ushered her into the sovereign's stall. Normally, the national anthem would then be sung. On this occasion, however, Doc H did not realize that the Queen was in her stall and went on playing the voluntary. His assistant was supposed to look over the top of the organ screen and tell the organist when to play the national anthem. But it seems he wasn't looking. The Queen waited in her stall; we all waited in our seats. And still the organ roared on. The dean in desperation shouted out loudly, 'The national anthem,' but the organist couldn't hear and played on. White to the gills by this time, the dean advanced a little further into the quire and cried out even louder, 'The national anthem.' This time, the organist did hear, stopped playing and started the national anthem. We shall never know whether perhaps the Queen giggled to herself about this.

On 17th March 1962, I was confirmed in the Anglican Church by the Bishop of Buckingham. The service took place in the quire of the chapel. I have a copy of the New Testament from *The New English Bible* inscribed by my parents to mark the occasion. I am not entirely sure at what point in my life I began to question my faith, if any, but confirmation of boys of my age was expected and not questioned. It was simply the norm, especially for the son of a clergyman and a chorister of St George's Chapel.

I think my doubts came to the surface when I went to public school at Marlborough College and started to think seriously, in my teens, about the meaning of life. I struggled with my beliefs and the expectations of others, concluding long ago that I was an atheist. I have often discussed religion – one of the three subjects traditionally barred from dinner-party conversation – and some years ago I read a wonderful book by journalist Lee Strobel called *The Case for a Creator*. However, my beliefs have not changed, although there are times, in the autumn of my life, when I wish that I could be convinced that there is a god. Interestingly, Lee Strobel later wrote: 'My road to atheism was paved by science...but, ironically, so was my later journey to God.'

Doc H retired in 1961. Besides his achievements as a choir trainer, he is best remembered today as a prolific composer of church music, his best-known work being 'Faire is the Heaven', composed in 1925. He composed for the Three Choirs Festival and the Proms, tutored Princess Elizabeth and Princess Margaret, was the musical director of many royal occasions and was a conductor at both the 1937 and 1953 coronations. He was knighted in 1954 and died in 1973, aged ninety.

Doc H was succeeded by Dr Sidney Campbell, who remained in office until his death in 1974. The choristers regarded him as something of a taskmaster and I suspect that he was not always able to bring out the best in his pupils. Sidney Campbell may have had his shortcomings but he was a very amusing character and an outstanding organist.

The choir sang regularly in the presence of the Queen and royal family and at the annual service of the Order of the Garter at the beginning of June, at the Royal Maundy in 1959 and at other significant events, including royal weddings, funeral services and thanksgiving services. At the Royal Maundy service, the Queen distributed specially minted silver coins, a set of which was presented to me. From time to time, we broadcast on BBC radio and television. There is a television recording of at least one service at which, as head chorister, I read a lesson, but I have yet to track this down.

The Garter Day was, and still is, a very grand affair when the Queen and Knights of the Garter process in velvet robes, glistening insignia and plumed hats, accompanied by a marching band and Officers of the Order, all in ceremonial dress, from the castle to the chapel where new Companions of the Order are installed. The route of the procession is lined with Life Guards from the Household Cavalry in their silver cuirasses, some of whom collapse from time to time in the heat and are carted off.

My parents were allocated tickets and invited family and friends, some of whom were seated in the chapel, others lining the route outside. They hosted a big tea party for about thirty people afterwards. As a chorister, I was in the chapel for the service before setting off down the steps back to school. However, after I left St George's School in 1963, I joined the Garter Day party as part of the family, all dressed up in my suit and tie.

In 1962, the dean, by then Robin Woods, and Sidney Campbell wanted to appoint me as head chorister. However, the headmaster of St George's School, William Cleave, had different ideas; I believe he may have felt that my family circumstances already imbued me with sufficient privilege. He was intent on appointing Soames Summerhays, who I believe was one of his favourite pupils. I believe there was quite a row between the chapel functionaries and the headmaster, the upshot of which was that Soames and I were appointed joint head choristers, a new head chorister's medallion being cast for the second position. We alternated between decani (on the dean's or south side of the quire) and cantoris (on the cantor's or north side of the quire). The appointment of head chorister was largely based on seniority and performance. We enjoyed certain privileges but our main responsibility was to lead, guide and set an example to other choristers, especially new members of the choir.

Shortly after I left St George's School, Clement McWilliam, assistant choirmaster and my music teacher, suggested we should make a recording of me singing some of the many solo pieces which I had sung in the chapel. He set up a 'studio', with a piano and tape recorder, in the drawing room of his house in the cloisters. After a little practice, we began recording. Sadly, however, my voice was already beginning to break and I simply could not achieve the pitch or tone that was expected. As far as I know, there is no surviving recording of me singing, except perhaps in the depths of the BBC or Independent Television (ITV) archives. There are certainly recordings of television and radio broadcasts but whether they are discoverable is another story.

23

*

I have never been a lover of boarding school but managed at St George's. I cannot say that I enjoyed it but I don't think that I disliked it, as I did my time at public school. The set-up at St George's was reasonably comfortable – as boarding schools go – and of course I was very close to home.

There were two or three dormitories, each with about thirty beds, and one small dormitory with four or five beds. I am not sure how one 'qualified' for this rather special dormitory but I was lucky enough to spend one or two terms there with friends. We had fun, especially peeping through the high-level window and watching the assistant matron, Mrs Elliot, in the bath – a time-honoured ritual, apparently. Bathrooms were, of course, communal with no hope of any privacy except in the loo.

I have memories of lying in bed in one of the larger dormitories and listening to the evocative sound of bell-ringing practice every Monday or Tuesday (I forget) from a nearby church – or perhaps it was from the Curfew Tower in the castle, a few hundred feet up the hill. The sound of church bells has always aroused in me a strong emotional response – some kind of nostalgia and the melancholy I have mentioned before.

There was also one night of big excitement as an intruder was spotted on the paths and steps leading from the school up to the castle. The police were called and numerous powerful torches scanned the hillside for any sign of life. We were all out of our beds, watching through the tall dormitory windows. I am not sure how the incident ended but no doubt the matron cajoled us all back into bed.

William Cleave – or Bill Cleave, as he was known – served as headmaster from 1946 until 1971. Regarded by some as a fine headmaster – and twenty-five years in the post would tend to support this view – I think he was widely disliked. I thought he was a bully and intimidated the boys, often with threats of corporal punishment of which he was a keen advocate. His wife, Peggy, was a very dominant woman and was not very popular either. Apparently, like *les tricoteuses* in the French Revolution, hanging around the guillotine waiting for heads to roll, she witnessed the canings while continuing to knit her woolly jumpers.

Bill Cleave was the principal teacher of French and he certainly managed to drum the basics into all of us. Every pupil dreaded French lessons; woe betide anyone who could not engage in conversation in perfect French. He made us all keep a hardback notebook, which we were instructed to call 'Conversational Gambits'. I still have this on my bookshelf today.

'Nourse, translate the next passage,' the headmaster ordered, and I struggled to come up with the correct pronunciation in French for 'grandson'.

'*Petit fils.* Repeat, *petit fils*,' he said. '*Fils* sounds like "peace".' I have never forgotten.

He also taught us carpentry in a well-equipped workshop where we created all sorts of useful items. I made a toast rack, among other things, which I gave to my parents who used it for many years. Compared with the horrors of the French classroom, I think we all enjoyed carpentry lessons.

I regularly won the Kempthorne Neatness Prize for my hand-writing and presentation of written work. The prize was usually one of the books from The Observer's Books series. The only one I can find in my bookshelf is *The Observer's Book of Architecture*, presented to me on 26th July 1962.

Despite my misgivings about Bill Cleave, he generally gave me good, and surprisingly perceptive, end-of-term reports. In my last report, for the Easter term, 1963, he wrote:

I'm glad that his final report is such a good one. I felt, as we all did, that he had it in him to do well and it is nice to know that we were

right. He has been most useful and helpful this term.
All good luck to him at Marlborough.

Sidney Campbell, master of the choristers, also gave me glowing reports.

As a minor canon of St George's Chapel, my father was expected to take on additional duties and so he taught part-time at the school. I was in his scripture class. In one report, he wrote, 'This is obviously not his strong subject.' He was right, despite my upbringing in a clergy household and exposure to the scriptures every day of my singing life. He also taught me Latin and English at some point.

He became very close friends with Francis Fewtrell, who taught me Latin, and Clement McWilliam, a delightfully unconventional and brilliant musician who supervised my piano lessons. Under his tutelage, I progressed through the Associated Board of the Royal Schools of Music exam grades, finally reaching Grade 6 (or higher) at Marlborough. He also taught me the clarinet. I am not exactly sure how I came to learn the clarinet but I must have expressed interest in learning at some point because my father presented me with a new clarinet (in a rather unpleasant tan-coloured case). I remember feeling disappointment because I would prefer to have played a stringed instrument, but I never told my parents and in fact went on to play in the school orchestra and in a brass and woodwind band called 'Brasser' at Marlborough.

When Clement was my teacher, I became interested in composing and spent a lot of time at the piano creating what were probably rather naive pieces, including one based on Benjamin Britten's *The Little Sweep*, an opera for young people. Later, during my time at Marlborough and university, I composed a number of pieces for the piano and voices, and one for the guitar, which could probably best be described as a dirge.

I recall that Francis, Clement and my father behaved rather like irrepressible schoolboys with an unusual gift for comic disruption, frequently taking the mickey out of their superiors and functionaries of the chapel. There is a story that Clement introduced a colleague – perhaps even my father, who was not very adventurous when it came to 'foreign' food – to the delights of Indian cuisine. Returning merrily to the castle, where he also lived, from the town below with a supply of uneaten chapattis, he proceeded to post them through the letterboxes of various priestly and official characters who lived in the cloisters.

I was lucky to have had Clement McWilliam as a teacher. He had a deep and unpatronizing insight into the minds of young people, at the same time insisting on the highest standards. He taught me for most of my time at St George's. Later in life, he became a brother at the Hospital of St Cross in Winchester where he died in July 2007.

Francis Fewtrell taught me Latin and he also supervised sports. He too was a character and I think most pupils wondered where his sexual proclivities lay. He was very tactile with the boys and was known for playing 'pocket billiards' in class – hands in his trouser pockets and a good deal of agitation! Nonetheless, he was a fine man and an excellent Latin teacher. His wife, Margery, was a good friend of the family too.

I must also mention Arthur Brown, Tony Kelly and Miss Blondin. They were not really part of the 'terrible trio' but deserve a mention as they were very much part of my school life.

Arthur taught maths, often showing off how he could work out arithmetic sums backwards. His tendencies were also questionable and he obviously enjoyed dispensing his own form of punishment, the 'Brixham'. This involved bending a boy over his knee, pulling up his shorts as high as possible and delivering an almighty slap with the palm of his hand.

In one class, one of the boys farted. Arthur detected the odour and asked the guilty party (not me!) to own up. Of course, nobody owned up, the consequence being that every member of the class was given a 'minus'. (Pluses and minuses were points dispensed to reflect good or bad behaviour and were read out by the headmaster at assembly every Saturday morning.) The following Saturday, we awaited with trepidation the outcome of this mass handing-out of minuses. I do not recall exactly what happened but, astonishingly, I think our beloved headmaster actually laughed at the absurdity of Arthur's punishment. Much to our relief, no further action was taken.

After Arthur Brown retired from teaching, he was ordained and took various stipendiaries, including Rector of St Bartholomew the Great in Smithfield in the City of London between 1979 and 1991. I once saw him, when I was working near the City, riding his tricycle, for which he was famous, with dog collar and boater.

Tony Kelly taught me history. I remember being the laughing stock of the class – if not the school – when asked who was the Head of the Anglican Church, to which I replied, 'The Pope.' Tony Kelly remained friends with my father for the rest of his life and helped me find somewhere to live in Pimlico when I started working in the City in 1972.

Miss Blondin, known universally as Blondie, was the granddaughter of Charles Blondin, the famous tightrope walker who crossed the Niagara River in 1859. She taught the younger boys a variety of subjects and was certainly not our favourite teacher. She was the subject of much mirth, especially when a boy standing before her and anticipating her famous slap across the face ducked just in time – loss of face is perhaps the appropriate expression. I believe she continued to live near the school after retiring and died not too long ago at some monumental age.

In the afternoons, after morning classes, we played sports, mainly football in the winter and cricket in the summer. I played in the football 1st XI. We enjoyed matches with other prep schools, including Cheam School in Berkshire, where Prince Charles was a pupil and a member of Cheam's 1st XI football team. On one occasion, when playing Cheam at home with Prince Charles on the visiting team, I put my hand in the air to reach for the ball, which of course immediately resulted in a foul and a penalty. I have never understood what prompted me to make this extraordinary manoeuvre and I was mortified, especially as this foul took place in front of royalty.

I was never awarded football colours while at school – vetoed, I suspect, by Bill Cleave. However, in the next issue of the *St George's School Chronicle*, my name appeared as having been awarded colours – 'posthumously', so to speak. I think that Francis Fewtrell, who refereed football, may have played a part in this unusual decision.

During my time at St George's, I developed a keen interest in photography. My mother owned a Kodak Brownie 44B, a 127-film camera with variable aperture and shutter speeds, which I had persuaded her to buy. I showed her how to use it and she took hundreds of colour slides, which are still in my possession today (but yet to be properly sorted, catalogued and digitized). I was lucky enough to acquire a Zeiss Ikon Ikonta, a superb German bellows camera, which I suppose must have been bought for me by my parents. I spent a great deal of time taking black-and-white photographs and foolishly sold this camera to a friend at Marlborough for £5. I took this collection of photographs in a briefcase to Hong Kong in 1984, where I lived until 2017, with a view to sorting and mounting them on special black paper which I had bought for this purpose. They remain unsorted and unmounted to this day, although I occasionally need to rummage in the briefcase to find a particular photograph. (Some of the photographs in this book come from these two collections.)

I suspect that most of us retain very few, if any, of our friends from prep school; after all, I am now looking back more than fifty years. I never attended any of the St George's School Association reunions; partly, no doubt, through complete lack of interest in my younger years, but also because I went to Hong Kong in my thirties and was unable to join these annual events without sacrificing valuable leave time. In recent years, however, now that we are spending more time in London, I have made the effort – and plucked up the courage – to go to the annual reunion, usually held on a glorious day in July. When I attended my first reunion in 2018, I enjoyed a tour of the chapel, seeing areas I had never seen as a chorister, and met old friends whom I had not seen since the early 1960s, including Mark Piper, Christopher Evans, Tim Holbech, Sheffield Exham and Maurice Kenwrick-Piercy. This was a very special occasion and we have kept in touch since, exchanging amusing stories and photographs from our school days. I continue to attend the annual reunion.

During the late 1950s and early 1960s, we used to holiday in Bude, on the north coast of Cornwall, on Dartmoor in Devon, and in Wales and Scotland. My parents could certainly not afford overseas holidays. In fact, I did not venture across the English Channel until I was sixteen, when a school friend and I hitch-hiked round northern France for a few rather wet days; two forlorn figures pinning our hopes on a ride, but it seemed the French would willingly run over you before stopping.

We stayed in guesthouses in Bude on a half-board basis – dinner (perhaps high tea would be a more apt description), bed and breakfast. We stayed in Summerleaze Crescent, which overlooked a beach of the same name. Christopher and I used to have enormous fun in the sand dunes behind the beach, often playing the 'Army Game'. Like the 'Prince Game' and the 'Office Game', Christopher usually assumed the senior role, in this case the general, while I occupied some more junior rank. I think I used to drive the jeep as well.

We loved Bude, with its rugged coastline, stunning beaches, rock pools and The Breakwater stretching into the sea to Barrel Rock.

The Breakwater is a well-known landmark originally constructed in 1819 to protect the canal but rebuilt immediately following a storm in 1838. I have not revisited Bude for many years but the sun setting over Barrel Rock is an indelible memory for me.

In Devon, we used to stay in a four-bedroom farmhouse next to the Tavistock Inn in Poundsgate, a small village with one shop on the east side of Dartmoor National Park. There was no electricity and the rooms were lit by gas lamps. We explored the whole of Dartmoor and spent many a happy day striding across the moors or building dams in the streams before enjoying a picnic lunch. Sometimes, Christopher and I would walk across the adjoining field to collect a jug of unpasteurized milk from the local farm. My parents' families joined us from time to time and we would all sit together in the evenings playing games by gaslight.

My parents bought a Bluebird caravan, which accommodated the four of us and gave us great pleasure for two or three years. We toured Scotland, more often than not in rather wet summer weather. We had a wigwam, which we used as a loo. On one occasion, we ventured south on the Mull of Kintyre – presumably heading for Campbeltown for old times' sake. Unfortunately, we ran out of petrol, which caused Mother to fly off the handle. We had a great deal of fun with the caravan but it all became too much work and it was sold to my father's sister, Aunty Mary.

We enjoyed some marvellous holidays in Scotland, my mother's home country. In 1960 (or 1961), my parents took a cottage on the Isle of Mull, off the west coast of Scotland. We took the car on the ferry from Oban on the mainland to Tobermory and then drove to the house. We were all a little shocked when we entered the house. Perhaps fortunately, the owner could not be present and had left the key. The state of the house was appalling: torn curtains, a broken toilet seat and a general air of neglect.

'Right, we are not staying here,' my father barked. He was

incensed and immediately telephoned the owner to say that we were leaving and that a refund would be demanded. (Whether this was ever forthcoming I do not know.)

'This is an absolute disgrace,' my mother added, as Christopher appeared before us carrying a forlorn-looking loo seat! We had to laugh.

We immediately returned to Oban and stayed in a hotel. My father telephoned the diocesan bishop to ask if there were any church livings available for a few weeks, our own holiday having been aborted. And so it was that we went to Moffat, an attractive town in Dumfriesshire (now Dumfries and Galloway), where Father took over the duties of the incumbent rector who was much in need of a holiday. We spent two or three years enjoying holidays in Moffat.

We would drive north in the gunmetal-grey Sunbeam Talbot, towing the small sailing dinghy, *Falcon*, on which Christopher and I learned to sail. We used to sail on the Thames at Bourne End but in Moffat we sailed on St Mary's Loch, half an hour's drive from the rectory where we were staying. We also used to walk up the surrounding hills, Saddle Yoke being one that remains vivid in my memory.

One of my mother's two sisters would often accompany us on holidays – but never at the same time, which would have undoubtedly led to a sisters' row. When Aunty Peggy accompanied us, her husband, Walter, would join us until he died in 1967. Walter was a very old-fashioned, fastidious man who invariably wore a three-piece, brown tweed suit, even in the heat of summer. He spoke with a broad Yorkshire accent and worked for Rowntree's. I don't think he had a very important job but he always brought Christopher and me a box of Rowntree's goodies comprising Kit Kat, Aero, Smarties, Rolo and Quality Street. Walter had an unfortunate habit of huffing and puffing while drumming his fingers and humming in a very funny manner, which I find hard to describe. Needless to say, Christopher and I – and I think probably

Father too – used to get the giggles while my mother would tick us off with silent words and stern faces.

On one occasion at lunch, Walter pressed my father to have more potatoes. 'John, will you have some more potatoes?'

'No, thank you,' replied my father.

'Are you sure?'

'I am quite sure, thank you,' my father replied sternly.

'But you must, there are only two left,' Walter countered.

At this point, my father slammed his fist on the table. 'I do not want any more potatoes,' he declared.

Silence followed.

Aunty Bunty, my mother's other sister, would also come on holiday. She had a son, Ronald, who also appeared from time to time. We got on well. Bunty was a widow and probably more fun than Peggy but all three sisters seemed to have endless rows – not speaking to one another for days at a time, if not longer. None of the sisters would ever walk or involve themselves in any activity, so my father, Christopher and I used to set off up a mountain or take out *Falcon* while my mother and whichever sister was in residence would sit for hours near the car, drinking tea and reading the *Daily Mail*. Many years later, after my parents moved to Charing, Bunty went to live with them because she was finding it difficult to cope on her own.

Since the early 1960s, my parents had been looking for a house to buy. As a priest, my father had always had housing provided but, looking to the future, he felt it was important to own a property. At this stage, the main focus was on acquiring a holiday home where the family could enjoy summers. Christopher and I were involved in some of the recces to Wales and the West Country.

One afternoon, shortly after I went to Marlborough, my parents turned up at the school on their way back to Windsor, obtained permission to meet me briefly and announced that they had bought a house in Devon: No 8, Burrow Road, Seaton, for which they paid £3,300. This was very exciting news and, in August 1963, we all moved into our new holiday home for four weeks.

The house formed part of a terrace of very ordinary houses. The front door opened into a hallway leading to a large kitchen at the end, with a living room and dining room on the right. Upstairs were four bedrooms and a bathroom. At the rear of the house was a west-facing patio with a small hut and the only door to the ground-floor loo.

Burrow Road runs north-south, perpendicular to the seafront and literally thirty yards from the esplanade. My bedroom was at the front of the house, facing east with a view of the sea to the south. I used to love having the window wide open at night and listening to the waves breaking on the pebble beach. Sometimes there was a storm – commonly known as a sou'wester – which had its own magic. I have always loved the sea and used to dream of having a small cottage on a cliff side, overlooking the sea and remote from the tribulations of everyday life – a lonely place to reflect on life. I still have this dream but I am old enough now to know it is unrealistic.

I have many happy memories of our holidays in Seaton, which we visited often throughout the year as well as for several weeks in the summer in the early years. Many friends and relations, including my father's brothers and sisters, Oswald, Mary and Morwenna, and cousins Frank and Sanchia, stayed with us. Peggy and Bunty were also regular visitors. On one particular occasion in the early days, Tooki, a friend of Christopher's, came to stay and I vividly recall the two of us talking late into the night as we painted the walls of the outside loo a sickly green.

I was scared out of my wits one night when the doorbell rang. My parents were in the kitchen and I opened the front door. Standing in front of me was an old man with a stick, dressed in a long mac and a cap. He looked menacing.

'Hello,' I said. 'Can I help you?'

He did not answer but gestured that he needed something – perhaps food or money. I shook my head and closed the door after watching him limp down the road, waving his stick about.

I was uneasy and went into the kitchen to tell my parents. Christopher appeared a little later and confessed all; it had been a prank. I have to admit that I would never have known that this seedy old man was Christopher in disguise. I was completely taken in, hook, line and sinker.

Almost on a daily basis, weather permitting, we used to establish ourselves at the Axe Yacht Club, a few minutes' walk from the house. My father, Christopher and I sailed regularly, sometimes on the river if the tide was high, and spent a lot of time 'simply messing about in boats', as Rat so sagely put it in *The Wind in the Willows*.

Christopher and I came across a tiny decrepit-looking boat in the harbour – obviously abandoned – and decided to 'appropriate' it. We immediately set about repairing it, hoping that it would not sink when first put to sea. The pram, which we named *Beanpod*, was launched, and Christopher paddled confidently out into midstream and managed to return without capsizing or sinking. A few months later, the true owners of the boat found us in the harbour, quite by chance, and reclaimed it. It was an embarrassing moment but we got away with it, pointing out that they had retrieved a much-improved, newly renovated boat.

A second sailing boat, *The Vital Spark*, which was larger than *Falcon*, was bought in early 1964. It seemed to have one problem after another, not least taking in water – probably because it was clinker-built. On one occasion, Father, Christopher and I launched the boat into a choppy sea, only to find that the centreboard jammed and we drifted rapidly towards a metal sewer pipe, which had substantial iron stanchions supporting it. We had to 'abandon ship' before watching the boat being battered against the steel posts and starting to sink. Fortunately, we were wearing life jackets and we managed to haul the boat to shore, where we found that the bottom had been holed. A number of spectators had gathered and offered help. I think the three of us felt a little embarrassed. We sold the boat a year later as it was very heavy to manoeuvre and had not been altogether satisfactory.

Other than sailing, we enjoyed relaxing in the sun. We also did a good deal of walking across the wonderful Devon cliffs. Another regular haunt was the Harbour Inn, a traditional pub dating from the twelfth century, situated on the River Axe just one mile from Seaton.

Whenever we left Seaton after our holidays, I was always sad and used to hum a little ditty I had composed about the river and the sea. We enjoyed Seaton for twenty years, although as Christopher and I grew up and started working, our visits were less frequent. The house was sold in July 1982 for £26,500.*

---

*   *In today's market, the property would be worth in the region of £300,000.*

Chapter 3
The Swinging Sixties

1963-1967

In the summer of 1963, aged thirteen, I found myself thrown into life at an English public school – Marlborough College in Wiltshire. My paternal grandmother had died a year or so before. My father interrupted my clarinet practice while I was still at St George's to break the news. It was my father's inheritance from my grandmother that enabled me to go to Marlborough; I had already unsuccessfully auditioned for a music scholarship at Wellington College. Founded in 1843 for the sons of Church of England clergy, bursaries were available and, with the assistance of my grandmother's estate, I was accepted. Unfortunately, Christopher did not benefit from her estate as he had already gone to school at Hurstpierpoint College, one of the famous Woodard schools.

My time at Marlborough, from 1963 to 1966, was not a happy period of my life. I found it difficult to acclimatize to the barren surroundings, the hollow echoing passages and the incessant noise of boys living in spartan surroundings. I vividly recall my father dropping me off outside A2 House, a junior house, and my entering a building which reminded me of a prison: a house with a central void looking down to the basement where tuck boxes and the like were stored. He later wrote to me to express his admiration for showing 'such great fortitude'.

I was well used to dormitories and communal bathrooms but, increasingly, I found the lack of any privacy and the daily regimentation very difficult. At the beginning of every term, we had to attend the weigh-in – lined up, completely naked, in the school sanatorium for weighing in and a visual inspection. I dreaded it every term.

The housemaster in A2 was called John Isaacson. He was known as 'Bum-eye' for reasons I don't know. (I am not sure of the spelling or meaning; according to the Urban Dictionary, 'a welling of the flesh around the eyes until the upper half of the face resembles the buttocks' – perhaps an appropriate description!) He was actually a good man and pretty fair as a housemaster.

I spent three terms in junior house and was promoted to head of house in my last term. John Isaacson felt that I had leadership qualities and he was right to encourage my talents. This was important to me. I became a captain in my senior house but never achieved prefect status.

As a former chorister at Windsor, I was of course immediately press-ganged into the chapel choir. Under the baton of the music director, Anthony Smith-Masters, the choir performed to a very high standard, singing at Sunday services and many other events. ABS, as he was known, also taught me the piano, continuing the good work of Clement McWilliam at St George's School.

Robert Peel taught me the clarinet at Marlborough and he was keen for me to join 'Brasser', the brass and woodwind band he directed. I agreed and derived enormous pleasure from being part of an orchestra with a diverse repertoire embracing classical pieces, musicals and a variety of jazz.

The daily routine was humdrum: early wake-up, classes, chapel (on Sundays), sports in the afternoon, prep (homework), bed at 9.30 pm and, of course, three meals a day in Norwood Hall, a monstrosity built in 1959 to 'blend in' with the fine architecture of the school buildings.

The food was not too bad and I used to eat huge amounts of roast potatoes and fried eggs, rejected by the more discriminating diners at our table. Seventeen roast potatoes was my record. The head chef, Ron, was as thick as two short planks but a friendly soul. Apparently, he used to go out to the pub every Friday night and drink thirteen pints of beer. One of my friends, Tim, once complained to him about lack of service (in a school refectory!) to which he replied, 'Mate, I've only got two pair of 'ands.' Laughter followed.

On Sundays, we had a good deal of free time after chapel in the morning. It was a time for letter writing, bicycling, hobbies and catching up with work. However, the highlight of our Sunday afternoons in A2 House was tuning in to *Pick of the Pops* with Alan Freeman on the BBC's Light Programme (now Radio 2). The Beatles, of course, took pride of place with hits such as 'She Loves You', 'From Me to You' and 'Please Please Me', but we should not forget Cilla Black's 'Anyone Who Had a Heart', one of my all-time favourites, Gerry & The Pacemakers, Frank Ifield, Roy Orbison, Cliff Richard and many, many others. I don't think The Rolling Stones made an appearance until 1964, with 'It's All Over Now'. One of my other great heroines was Sandie Shaw, who also appeared in the charts in 1964 with 'Always Something There to Remind Me'. The list goes on and on; there were so many great artists performing memorable music, which is perhaps more than can be said of much of today's popular-music scene.

After junior school, I moved up to senior school in B3 House (now known as Morris House and home to about seventy girls). B3 was situated across the Bath Road, over the road from the main campus. Percy Chapman was the housemaster, a rather unprepossessing character who was nonetheless very astute and later retired to become parish priest of St Michael's Church in Aldbourne, a small village about six miles north-east of Marlborough.

He was succeeded by Jake Seymour, who was larger than life, full of innocent bluster, but a very caring person. He had served in the Sudan before independence in 1953. He taught many subjects including history, which I never mastered. At the beginning of one class, he told a boy, 'Do not come into my class with dirty shoes.' The boy was dispatched and returned shortly with shining black shoes. If only education today were as wide-ranging.

He also ran poetry competitions – presumably as part of English lessons – which I used to embrace enthusiastically. My poem, *Ode to Yasmina*, won first prize, which was half a crown. This was a lengthy poem, written in 1966 when I was sixteen, a small section of which I reproduce here.

> We suffered and we lived,
> We loved, such lovers.
> There was no scorn, but only tears, .
> Of tearful day;
> Or fear, and then a softly smile.
> There is no end, for life's eternity is heaven,
> And heaven is only love.
> And then we came, close and close, so close;
> The clasp was one forever.
> What passion in our lips,
> And burning hearts, enlightened love.
> One body, life, in mystic union,
> Driven wild in want.
> Oh, what ecstasy of bliss,
> In earthly transport, heavenly love.
> And then we sighed, with joy for life,

Still close;

Our minds in dreams of sleep,

Till parting, sleep of dreams did part us.

I was going through a very difficult and emotional stage of life, typical of so many teenagers. I spent much of my time in the school library reading and writing poetry in beautiful italic, with green ink, drawing sketches and displaying whatever artistic talents I might have possessed.

As part of our schoolwork, we undertook a number of projects of our own choosing. My enthusiasm for photography was growing and I had always been interested in architecture, so I went in search of contemporary buildings which I could write about and photograph. One of my findings was St Clement's Roman Catholic Church in Epsom, completed in 1962, which is a brick and concrete structure of very little merit, in my view, but so typical of the period.

Marlborough offered some flexibility in the daily routine and it was possible to spend an afternoon cycling – bicycles were known as 'grids' – instead of playing sport. I used to cycle off to nearby fields, buying a packet of Player's N°6 cigarettes from a friendly shop en route, and enjoy relaxing with a quiet smoke. On one occasion when I returned to school, I bumped into Mrs Wright, the wife of my chemistry teacher, who was always pleased to talk to me. There was indeed gossip about Mrs Wright and me. She obviously smelt cigarette smoke on my breath.

'Have you been smoking?' she asked.

'No,' I replied firmly and that was happily the end of the matter.

I also took up the guitar while in my senior house. I had no formal lessons and taught myself with the help of manuals and friends who played. I derived enormous pleasure from the guitar and would play all the popular songs – The Beatles' classics as well as many of Peter, Paul and Mary's favourites, including 'Puff, the

Magic Dragon', 'Lemon Tree', 'Where Have All the Flowers Gone?' and many more. I wrote one song, 'Wish You Hadn't Given Me the Things You Did', which perhaps reflected my rather rebellious nature. I am not sure that I can explain why I felt as I did, other than perhaps believing I wanted to be a 'man of the people', rather than a privileged public-school boy. Looking back, I cannot imagine why I should have had such absurd thoughts!

I had always wanted to become a doctor and this was also the assumption of the family. I therefore chose biology, chemistry and physics as my A-level subjects, all of which were required to gain a place to read medicine at university or enter medical school in those days. Today, I believe the subject requirements are a little more flexible, although very high standards are still required. I enjoyed these subjects and was fascinated by the human body. I recall vividly the smell of formaldehyde and dead rats, which we were required to dissect, and also the chemistry labs where we mixed up all sorts of chemicals, sometimes with alarming results. I was also very intrigued by physics, although this subject proved to be my downfall as I did not perform well in exams – least of all physics.

During what was to be my last term at Marlborough, the Michaelmas term of 1966, I was allocated Study 31 in New Court, a cloister within the school precincts, which I shared with Gerry Waddington and Johnny Reeve. I used to get up at about 5.30 every morning, go to my study, make a coffee and spend hours redrawing my biology sketches in enormous detail. I treasured these drawings for years; sadly, they were 'lost' during one of my father's clear-outs in later life.

We decided to keep a visitors' book to record the comments of our many guests. Looking through this book, which is still in my possession, I can see that we entertained well, although at the time I was struggling with a decision regarding my future at Marlborough. The book contains numerous entries, many amusing and some of the racy variety, from friends who visited for coffee and a chat. There were also quite a number of female visitors but I am not sure where they came from. There is one telling comment from my friend Malcolm, the Earl of Caithness, who wrote: 'Philip has taken the great decision...'

During this final year, after three years at Marlborough, I became increasingly unhappy and asked my parents if I could leave before my A levels. There were many discussions and my parents and Jake Seymour, my housemaster, did their best to persuade me to stay, but I think I was determined and, in the end, it was agreed that I should leave at the end of the Michaelmas term. There was a leaving party in my study on 15th December. Malcolm, my good friend who had written in our visitors' book, felt exactly the same way and left shortly after me. Later on, I questioned whether my parents had done the right thing allowing me to leave. There are times when I have looked back and felt that the decision was a weak one, but my parents were not the sort to make me stay on. I will never know what would have been best but I do not believe it affected my life adversely.

Although I was unhappy, I had some fun and made good friends, a few of whom I keep in touch with to this day. We do not meet very often but they have attended my significant birthday parties and we continue to exchange Christmas cards.

John Dancy was headmaster (or The Master, as the headmaster of Marlborough was known) throughout my time at Marlborough. In my last school report, he wrote:

> *...he became more settled as soon as the decision was taken to leave, and in the second half of term contributed quite a bit. But I don't for a moment imagine all his problems are now at an end, especially if he pursues the idea of reading psychology. If, however, he keeps his grip and is tough with himself, it could well be that in ten years' time he will be the stronger for his current tribulations.*

I remember John Dancy as a very fine man and a pioneering liberal educationalist who made a big contribution to the college's development. He was instrumental in starting the moves towards co-education and was a key member of the Public Schools Commission.

It was the very start of co-education at Marlborough and a prelude to the arrival of the first fifteen girls, who were admitted to the sixth form in 1968. I also recall John Dancy's lovely daughter, Nicola, who may have been involved in the initial co-educational experiment and visited our study a few times. John died, aged ninety-nine, on 28th December 2019.

I do not remember a huge amount about my schooldays; perhaps because I have never felt they were an important part of my life. This was brought home to me when I visited Marlborough in May 2017 for a fifty-year reunion. I met many of my peers who had vivid memories of our time at school – and one who was apparently my mentor. Others had clear memories of the rooms in which we lived and worked. I had surprisingly little recollection but was happy to be reawakened.

At the beginning of 1967, I began a new phase of my life at Davies, Laing and Dick, a private educational college, with a good reputation, where I could complete my A-level studies and be prepared for the examinations that I needed for admission to medical school. It could best be described as a crammer. The college was based in Pembridge Square in Notting Hill, London. Today, DLD, as it is now known, is a college with boarding facilities and offering a wide range of courses – a far cry from the primitive facilities of Pembridge Square more than fifty years ago.

I used to commute daily from Windsor and Eton Central station to Paddington, changing at Slough, and then take the Tube to Notting Hill Gate. I would travel home with a girl called Anne, who lived in Lower Shiplake, near Henley, and we would always try

My parents' wedding day, Glasgow, 18th May 1945

My grandmother with me, aged six months,
Bournemouth, 1950

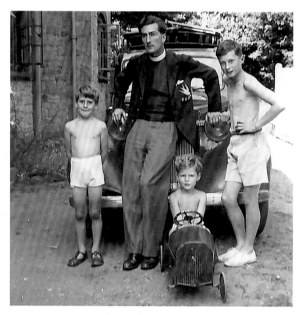

Christopher (left), my father and my cousin Ronald,
with me in the car, Peaslake, circa 1952

The Parsonage, Peaslake, 1956

St George's School, 1958 (I am circled, my father is in the dog collar front right)

From left: Me, neighbour Donald Fehrenbach, Ronald, my father and
Christopher at No 10 The Cloisters, Christmas Day 1960

In the school play, St George's School, 1961

St George's School, the Football 1st XI, 1961
(I am in the back row, third from right)

Our first house in Windsor Castle, No 10 The Cloisters, with the
Round Tower and St George's Chapel on the right, winter 1962-63

St George's Chapel choir, early 1960s (I am in the middle row, third from left)

Head chorister, St George's Chapel, 1963

From left: Christopher, Aunty Morwenna, me, my mother and my father
on the Esplanade at Seaton, 1964

'Brasser', the wind band at Marlborough College, circa 1965
(I am in the front row, second from right)

My parents' silver wedding
anniversary, Canterbury,
18th May 1970

Travelling home after a business trip
to the north of England, 1970s

On holiday in Cornwall, 1975

With Sarah, Teddington, 1984

to complete the *Evening News* crossword before we reached Slough, where I had to change for the branch line to Windsor. I quite enjoyed the new experience of commuting and, of course, my new freedom while living at home, after years of boarding school.

If I am honest, DLD did not benefit my academic performance but I was at least happier than I was at Marlborough. I sat my A levels in the summer of 1967 and did not excel myself: two C grades, in biology and chemistry, and a D in physics. Determined – or so I thought – to go to medical school, I later enrolled for an A-level course in physics at Llandaff Technical College, now known as Cardiff Metropolitan University, in South Wales, where I lived and worked for the best part of a year, working for Community Service Volunteers during my gap year. I was lucky to find a college which ran evening classes nearby and I attended twice a week after work. I sat physics A level once again and didn't do much better. I was not going to medical school.

Living in Windsor Castle was an extraordinary experience and a huge privilege. We were very fortunate in that we had access to the Home Park, which was entirely private. There is a golf course, where my father and I used to attempt to play a few holes; and Frogmore Cottage, the official UK residence of the Duke and Duchess of Sussex, also forms part of the estate.*

We often enjoyed strolls in the park, although Mother rarely joined us. She was not a walker. It was not uncommon to meet the Queen walking with her corgis.

'Good afternoon, Ma'am,' my father, Christopher and I would say in unison.

'Good afternoon, gentlemen,' the Queen would typically reply. 'Isn't it a lovely day?'

---

* *The Duke and Duchess of Sussex are now residing in California.*

'It is indeed, Ma'am,' Father would say, and then we would hurry along.

I suppose we all became rather blasé about meeting royalty.

How did I feel about living inside the walls of a royal castle where the Queen was often in residence, with the Royal Standard fluttering in the breeze on top of the Round Tower, and with VIPs attending ceremonies in St George's Chapel and other major events in the castle? Our encounters with the Queen and members of the royal family were, of course, infrequent – usually at royal parties held in the State Apartments. Nonetheless, we lived in awe of our surroundings and with a sense of incredulity. It was a fairy-tale way of life.

We also had access to the private section of Windsor Great Park, which covers nearly 5,000 acres and includes the Deer Park and the famous Savill Garden. If we were feeling energetic, Christopher and I used to walk to the Great Park along the Long Walk, an avenue running straight as a die for a little over two and a half miles south of the castle to the Copper Horse statue of King George III.

The family had many friends inside the castle, including the dean and canons and their families, the lay clerks, military knights and of course our good neighbour, Donald Fehrenbach.

Canon and Mrs Bentley (Nina), who lived at No 8 The Cloisters, had four children with whom Christopher and I were friends. From my bedroom window in our first house, No 10, I used to see their youngest daughter, Teresa, pottering about on the patio in front of her house. She was about fifteen and rather attractive in her short skirt. We wrote to each other while I was at Marlborough, where the Gonks she had made for me graced my study. Although the family left Windsor in 1967, Teresa and I must have kept in touch because, sometime in the mid-1980s, we had a fling.

Early in 2008, I bumped into her elder brother, Nic, who worked in Hong Kong. We were in the bar of the Hong Kong Club.

'Hello, Philip, what a surprise. How are you?' Nic said.

We sat in one of the bar's cubicles and exchanged the usual pleasantries and then Nic said, 'I think you should know that Teresa died in January.'

I was taken aback. I knew she was suffering from multiple sclerosis and was very upset to hear this news. 'What age was she?' I asked.

'She would have been sixty. To be honest, it was probably for the best; she no longer had any quality of life.'

Teresa's untimely death preyed on my mind for some time. We went back a long way – since 1957 – and I was very fond of her. And now she was gone.

My parents knew Viscount 'Bill' Slim and his wife, Aileen, who lived in a rather unusual apartment in the Norman Tower. Slim, who had a highly successful military career and is best known for his defeat of the Japanese in the Burma campaign in World War II, was Constable and Governor of Windsor Castle from 1964 until his death in 1970. We were occasionally invited to parties, including a lunch where I insisted on wearing a horizontally striped knitted tie – all the rage in the 1960s – much to the consternation of my mother, who thought it was inappropriate for such a formal occasion. She was probably right.

Christopher and I also used to visit Colonel Squibb, one of the military knights, and his wife, Kay. They lived in a small house in the Lower Ward, where all the military knights were housed. I am not sure how we came to meet the Squibbs but, in the early days, we used to pop in for a chat after taking Marcus, our golden retriever, for a walk. On one occasion, Marcus cocked his leg against the back of the armchair in which Mrs Squibb was sitting. She was unaware of what was happening; we said nothing and made a hasty exit!

The Squibbs consumed vast amounts of gin, starting as soon as the sun was over the yardarm and finishing sometime in the evening, with a brief post-prandial break. I suppose that we did not indulge in this pastime until we had at least reached our teens. We were then plied with drink and sometimes used to stagger home to No 10.

Christopher and I attended parties in the castle where we met all the royals. Prince Charles, who was less than a year older than I was, and Princess Anne, a year younger, hosted parties where we met the Queen, the Duke of Edinburgh, Princess Margaret, the Earl of Snowdon (Antony Armstrong-Jones) and many other dignitaries and important people. At this time, despite appearing to be happily married, Margaret and Antony's love story was marred by reports of multiple affairs. *The Daily Telegraph* wrote, 'Those close to the couple suggest Lord Snowdon was the first to be unfaithful' because, as a photographer, he took long business trips abroad. However, Margaret was also reportedly connected to several men while she was married. They were divorced in 1978.

At one party, I danced with Princess Anne and, trying to make polite conversation, said, 'I understand you are interested in horses.'

'Yes, I am… It's very warm in here. Let me go and arrange for a window to be opened.'

She made a hasty retreat and that was the last I saw of her that evening. I am not sure why my comment appeared to offend her.

We also became friends with a number of Eton College housemasters and their families. They all seemed to live in vast houses and Christopher and I attended many dances, usually organized by the daughter of the house.

At one such party, I met a girl called Monica Schmoller, who lived in the insalubrious town of West Drayton. We were both thirteen. We had several dances and I managed to bag her for the 'last waltz' at midnight, the traditional final dance at these parties when one had the chance for a cuddle and, if you were lucky, a kiss.

Christopher had arranged a party a few weeks later, to which

I was allowed to invite guests. So I sent Monica a formal invitation (as one did in those days):

Philip Nourse requests the pleasure of the company of Monica Schmoller...

Some days later, I received her formal reply:

*Monica Schmoller thanks Philip Nourse for his kind invitation but regrets that she is unable to accept...**

And at the bottom of the reply card:

* and is unlikely to be able to accept any future invitations.

I was mortified. Monica was hastily crossed off the guest list and I hid her reply card in a safe place. Thank heavens neither my parents nor Christopher ever saw her reply. I took this as a 'Dear John' and we did not meet again.

My first 'proper' girlfriend was called Philippa Simons, the younger sister of well-known BBC Radio broadcaster Susannah Simons. We met at a party in 1964 and went out together a few times. I have completely lost touch and have no idea where she is now. I believe she married a rather wealthy gentleman and went off to live in the Caribbean.

I then met Sara Fraser, an alluring girl, who was the younger daughter of my dentist's practice partner. The family lived in a lovely house in Burnham Beeches, Farnham Common, about twenty minutes' drive from Windsor. I used to go to the family house on most Sunday evenings to watch *The Forsyte Saga* accompanied by toast and boiled eggs. We went out for a year or two and had a great deal of fun during 1967, while I was living at home and attending Davies, Laing and Dick. A small group of us used to visit pubs, albeit we were underage, and go to friends' parties. I also remember walking through Burnham Beeches or along The Brocas by the River

Thames and listening to records in the sitting room of the quarters in which Christopher and I lived in the castle. Sara and I enjoyed spending time together on our own.

Nineteen sixty-seven was the Summer of Love – an extraordinary period of Dionysian culture, erasing the last dregs of the whisky-sipping *Mad Men* era and ushering in a new culture encompassing hippies, drugs and free love. Kipper ties, Chelsea boots, miniskirts for girls and John Lennon sunglasses, of course, were de rigueur. It is hard to describe the feelings that so many of us, aged seventeen or thereabouts, experienced but Scott McKenzie's chart-topping 'San Francisco (Be Sure to Wear Flowers in Your Hair)', written by John Phillips of The Mamas & The Papas (the single reportedly selling more than seven million copies worldwide), summed up the emotions of so many young people. A short time afterwards, The Beatles released 'All You Need Is Love', one of my all-time favourites.

Late that summer, Sara came up by train to stay for a week in a beautiful flat my parents had taken in North Berwick, a seaside town east of Edinburgh and overlooking the Firth of Forth. We spent much of our time walking along the beach, hand in hand, and exploring nearby haunts in the late-summer sunshine. When we took Sara to the train to go home, my mother came out with one of her classic remarks: 'Don't fall off the train.' This phrase was to be repeated many times, much to the amusement of us all.

It was here in North Berwick, on a cool and breezy beach, that I painted *Fidra*, one of my attempts at oils. It depicts this rocky island, home to a colony of puffins, with its prominent lighthouse against a grey, stormy sky. The island is said to have been the inspiration for Robert Louis Stevenson's *Treasure Island*. The name 'Fidra' is believed to come from Old Norse, referring to the multitude of bird feathers on the island.

This was a truly exciting time of life. I am not sure that I was happy within myself, but we had fun with friends. These were the days shortly before the breathalyser was introduced and I used to drive to and from parties in my father's car, which we would not even think of today.

But at home in my bedroom, I would sit at my desk late into the night, sometimes rather depressed and contemplating the world, analysing dreams and writing notes. I suspect that I may have had occasional suicidal thoughts too. My parents even took me to see my mother's psychiatrist, who promptly prescribed anti-depressants, or similar, but I am pretty sure it was a placebo. I kept a diary for some time but sadly destroyed it a few years later.

I have never understood why I felt as I did, although during my university years I was interested in undergoing psychoanalysis, which may have unearthed all sorts of secrets. I was just an emotional teenager – like so many others. Perhaps the words of John Dancy, my headmaster at Marlborough, were percipient: 'I don't for a moment imagine all his problems are now at an end, especially if he pursues the idea of reading psychology.'

My relationship with Sara began to fizzle out when I headed off to Cardiff to work in the autumn of 1967. We kept in touch but in 1968 she married a rather short man called Mike, who asked Christopher to be his best man. I perhaps felt a little piqued but then why would I be involved, as the ex-boyfriend?

Also during that wonderful summer, Sylvie, a French girl and sister of Michele, who had stayed with us some years earlier in Peaslake, came to stay with us, supposedly to learn English. Sylvie was my age, slender with sultry good looks, long dark hair, soulful eyes and Cupid's bow lips. She looked every inch the chic French girl.

My parents had a frightful row during lunchtime on the day of her arrival and my father actually stood up and tipped over the table, sending plates, cutlery and raspberry jelly in all directions. Father marched off, Christopher stormed out of the front door, kicking empty milk bottles down Denton's Commons, while my mother and I tried calmly to pick up the pieces. To this day, I am not sure how we managed to restore equilibrium and welcome our new guest.

Sylvie and I became very close and spent a great deal of time together. She came from a well-to-do Parisian family who lived at one of the best addresses and spent summers on the French Riviera. She was duly impressed by staying in Windsor Castle and attending a grand concert in the deanery on her first night, cocktail parties and other events. She also met many of our friends. Sylvie returned to see us in 1969 in Canterbury, where we were by then living, and the family decamped to our holiday house in Seaton. I think she was a little shocked at the ordinariness of our terraced house. Nonetheless, we had enormous fun and usually went to bed very late, long after my parents and Christopher had retired. A few weeks later, Sylvie and I returned to Canterbury *à deux* before she went home to Paris. Although we corresponded for a few months, I never saw her again and never understood what had gone wrong. But I was nineteen. Sylvie was an important person in my life, someone I have not forgotten.

Christopher and I had so many friends, some of whom I still keep in touch with. As recently as 2020, Vicki, a very old friend who was one of the Farnham Common crowd and lived in a beautiful house, sent me a card in which she enclosed a black-and-white photograph of me, dressed in morning coat and with long wavy hair, at her wedding on 21st October 1972 – my twenty-third birthday.

In 1967, my father was advised by Robin Woods, the dean, that it was time to move on from Windsor. Most minor canons did a stint of five years; my father had done ten.

'Look, you may think it's jolly good being here and all that, but the fact is that you are not stretched enough,' the dean told my father. 'Really, you need to get your teeth into a proper job; this isn't enough of a job for you.'

My father was alarmed and my mother certainly did not want to leave Windsor. After looking at many livings, Father accepted the offer to become Vicar of Amesbury.

Ten years and ten months on, my parents packed up and very sadly left Windsor Castle. They drove out through the Henry VIII Gateway for the last time, the familiar policemen saluting, and set off for a new life in Wiltshire at the Abbey Church of St Mary and St Melor, Amesbury. I was in Cardiff at the time and missed the move.

My parents were reluctant to make the move to Amesbury but I know my father was impressed by the magnificent abbey church and excellent choir. There were remains of the abbey cloisters and various remnants of chapels and chantries. Amesbury was a rather unprepossessing town, famous for Stonehenge and close to Boscombe Down, a Ministry of Defence air station where my father was officiating chaplain.

I only stayed in Amesbury occasionally as I was living in Cardiff and then went off to university.

Chapter 4
Uxbridge not Oxbridge

1967-1972

Having failed to achieve the A-level grades required for medical school, I decided to read psychology at university, despite the misgivings voiced by John Dancy in my final school report. However, in the 1960s, gaining a university place was highly competitive, especially for courses in social sciences and related subjects. The Universities Central Council on Admissions (UCCA) was therefore formed to manage the increase in university applications and effectively provide a central clearing house for those students who had not already received an offer of a place. Since A-level results were not published until August each year, it was not possible for me to apply for Voluntary Service Overseas (VSO) for my gap year, as I would have liked.

I therefore applied for a position with Community Service Volunteers (CSV), a UK-based volunteering organization founded by Robert Davies, which offered high-quality volunteer programmes in a wide variety of communities. I was posted to Cardiff where I was responsible for managing a team of volunteers and an administration office, reporting to Robert Davies, a wonderful man whom I admired enormously; he was animated by and committed to a strong desire to serve the community.

The following is a short extract from a handwritten letter, dated 15th October 1967, from Robert Davies to a friend (which I came across on the Internet):

The full-time volunteer from Community Service Volunteers arrived last Wednesday and I took a half-day leave to meet him. He actually comes from Windsor and the Castle itself, where his father is some sort of Chaplain, and he went to Marlborough College. However, neither seem to be any disadvantage and I am sure he will prove himself well-suited to the job.

Finances, I am glad to say, are now such that we have been able to fix him up with a good landlady (!) at 5 gns/wk and can maintain the weekly 30/- pocket money plus 10/- expenses. So actually he is receiving the equivalent of £7.5s per week which is not bad at eighteen!*

Having managed two months without full-time help, all those who have worked on rota part-time are expecting to be suddenly relieved from their burdens. I am therefore fighting to protect him from being exploited. We have been extra busy in the last three months because of under-recruitment in the Police Force and the absence of a police cadet. Since last week we now have another. The Chief Inspector in charge is so keen that he is detailing them all to attend the main part of our Conference at the end of the month...

---

* *In pre-decimal currency, there were 20 shillings in a pound. £7.5s is equal to £7.25 in decimal currency (introduced in 1971).*

I did indeed have a good landlady in the form of Mrs Evans, who lived with her husband in a small terraced house in Cowbridge Road East. There were two other lodgers, Pete and Martin, who were both students at the university. Mrs Evans was very kind to me but I have to say I did not like being served 'dinner' when I got home at about 5.00 pm.

She would call up to my bedroom, 'Philip, your dinner is on the table.'

I would reluctantly descend and dig into my 'high tea', which was all over twenty minutes later, making the evenings rather long.

I wanted more independence and found myself new digs in Sophia Close, overlooking Sophia Gardens and just five minutes' walk from my office at No 2 Cathedral Road. I had a rather large room and our hosts served dinner at 7.00 pm. There were a number of older and interesting lodgers who joined the evening meal, including a very erudite retired teacher with whom I had many discussions.

This was in May 1968 at the time of the 'revolutionary' Paris riots, which led to civil unrest throughout France and lasted for almost two months. I remember watching street battles between students and police in the Latin Quarter of Paris on the television news, scenes which today would seem unremarkable. There was plenty for an eighteen-year-old and a retired teacher to deliberate over.

Some ten months working with CSV among the poor and disadvantaged in some of the most impoverished areas of Cardiff was a sobering experience and an eye-opener. I had seen depressed areas of London when a friend and I used to make special trips to poor areas to see 'real life', and when we also attended a week's course in East London to gain an insight into what was then a very impoverished area of the capital. That, of course, has all changed with gentrification over the past twenty or so years.

But in Cardiff, I came face to face with people in need, a completely new experience. I myself visited lonely people living in appalling conditions – sometimes with few possessions, often talking to themselves or hallucinating. Besides the elderly and the lonely, I came across people with mental-health issues or problems with drugs or alcohol. Sometimes, we needed to call in healthcare professionals. It was my job to provide whatever help we could with a team of remarkable and dedicated volunteers. This might be in the form of physical assistance – shopping, cleaning, redecorating – or simply being with them, talking, caring and arranging community events. The response from these lonely people was extraordinary – an appreciation that few of us can imagine.

We also arranged trips to schools and conferences in order to promote the importance of charitable work in the community. The organization, now known as VCS Cymru, is today the oldest volunteer bureau in the UK and works closely with the United Nations Association Exchange to keep the international volunteering tradition alive.

Although I was assuming a lifestyle quite different from anything I had experienced before, I embraced the day-to-day challenges with commitment and passion, ready to take responsibility and do whatever was necessary. It was hugely rewarding.

In August 1968, I was offered a place at Brunel University in Uxbridge, London, to read my chosen subject, psychology (with social sciences). This was a four-year sandwich course, with three work placements, leading to a bachelor's degree with honours. Although I was a little daunted by the prospect of four years at university, I relished the idea of working in the summer – and it proved to be a remarkable opportunity to undertake projects of almost any sort, so long as there was some relevance to the degree course.

I arrived for my first term in late September. Despite having spent the best part of a year in Cardiff, where I encountered so many different people, I was surprised by the diversity of my fellow students, who came from all sorts of backgrounds and ethnicities.

I realized how little I really knew about mixing with people who had not been to private schools; and after a period of acclimatization, I began to involve myself in a new life.

Ironically, the first person I met and became friends with was from Harrow public school. I was queuing up for dinner in the refectory during the first week at university and this complete stranger opened a conversation with me.

'My name's Robert Atkinson. Which football team do you support?'

'I don't,' I replied tersely.

Well, Robert was a manic supporter of Newcastle United – and even today I still don't know the difference between the Premier League and a League Championship. We somehow clicked and the rest is history. We remained the closest of friends throughout his life – through good times and bad. Robert was posted to Hong Kong in the early 1980s and, almost by chance, I was to follow him in 1984.

Robert and I also became close friends with Ian Anderson and Chris Bell, both of whom I keep in touch with to this day. Robert, Ian and Chris were all reading psychology, sociology and economics, a combined degree, so we rarely came across one another other than at some psychology lectures, but we met up regularly for libation and at mealtimes. Robert, an advocate of European integration, joined an accountancy firm before switching career to banking and ultimately joining the diversified Swire Group. Chris found his feet in criminology and became a successful solicitor. Ian was a great ideas man and revelled in economic philosophy. He made his career in hospital management, having long before failed to fulfil his dream of becoming an airline pilot.

I also met a very interesting mature student called Neville Symington, also a psychology student, who was part of the famous Symington family who owned several vineyards in Portugal famous for their port and Madeira wine. He was a tall man with wispy hair

and spoke in measured tones with a slight lisp. He was formerly a
Catholic priest, who lost his faith and turned to psychoanalysis. After
graduation, he went on to become a very distinguished psychoanalyst
and a prolific writer. Sadly, we lost touch. However, while writing these
words, I managed to track down a friend of his on Facebook, who told
me that Neville had died in Sydney, where he had emigrated in the
1980s, in December 2019.

One of the highlights of our humdrum routine was walking up
the hill to The Red Lion in Hillingdon, or *Le Lion Rouge* as we called
it, where we would each buy half a pint of beer and put the world to
rights before returning for supper in the refectory. In my first year,
I was living in lodgings in Gerrards Cross, so I would return home
after supper on my Honda 50 motorbike or in Christopher's Morris
Minor, which I borrowed for a time.

Following my musical upbringing, I also joined the Brunel
orchestra in which I led the percussion section, relishing in the
power of the timpani as well as tenderly stroking the triangle from
time to time. Our first performance was Mussorgsky's *Pictures at
an Exhibition*. I remember having fun and laughing a good deal –
perhaps because the orchestra was just so *bad*.

Much as I disliked the environment of Brunel University and
its Brutalist architecture – the lecture-theatre block was designated
as a Listed Building Grade II in 2011 – I was impressed by the
academic standards and approach to teaching. I was certainly
a great deal more motivated than I was at Marlborough and
immersed myself in my studies, which included all branches of
psychology, sociology, anthropology and Bayesian statistics. The
principal psychology lecturer was Dr Larry Phillips, an American
academic educated at the University of Michigan, who was a good
teacher and tutor. We were not overstretched with numerous
lectures, much of our study being undertaken individually in the
university library or elsewhere.

*

Although I was never directly affected, it was during this time that 'The Troubles' in Northern Ireland began. Every day, the news was dominated by the violence taking place, which included terrorist attacks in London. The conflict was primarily political and nationalistic in nature and, of course, provided ripe material for heated discussion in student seminars.

The Northern Ireland Conflict, as it was known internationally, was a violent sectarian conflict involving the mainly Protestant loyalists, who wanted the province to remain part of the United Kingdom, and the overwhelmingly Roman Catholic republicans, who wanted it to become part of a united Ireland. The confrontation, marked by sensational bombings and other forms of terrorism, had the characteristics of a civil war and resulted in more than 3,500 deaths and over 30,000 wounded before a peaceful power-sharing solution was agreed in 1998.

During my second term at Brunel in January 1969, my father was appointed Precentor of Canterbury Cathedral, the senior cathedral in the Anglican Church throughout the world. My parents had never really been happy at Amesbury; they did not care for it as a place and my mother hated it. My father had been casting about wildly to find another living after a mere six months in Amesbury and it happened that the precentorship of Canterbury became vacant. So they moved from a rather comfortable six-bedroom house, where I had a large top-floor bedroom, to a somewhat dark and cramped fifteenth-century house in the precincts of the cathedral. My mother had apparently said that she did not mind what the house was like 'as long as we can get out of Amesbury'. Once again, I had a top-floor bedroom – considerably smaller, I should add, than that in Amesbury – but I did not spend a great deal of time at home.

Because the house was so cramped, the piano had to be placed in a rather strange area – apparently an old bakery – at the end of a long passage. When I was at home during university holidays, I spent a great deal of time here playing the piano and trying to compose various pieces of liturgical music, one of which was a hymn called 'Son of Man'. I believe I may have sent this off to my father's publisher, Josef Weinberger, who had published a piece called 'We're All for Thee, Lord' in 1970. If I did, I don't think I heard anything further. Like some of my other 'works', I still have the words and score in my file at home. Music has always been an important part of my life but moving on from school and away from home made it much more difficult to play, except for those occasions when I was at home.

Around this time, I also wrote another poem to add to my small collection:

The Day

Each dawn awakes, a newborn peace;
Forgotten dreams, forgotten grief;
The day grows old,
I grow less bold;
Then dusk arrives;
My heart, it cries,
But never dies.

The Brunel University sandwich course worked on the basis of two terms in residence and the summer term replaced with a work placement. Students generally found placements for themselves but, of course, they had to be approved by their tutors.

For my first work placement in 1969, I secured a position in market research, based in London, interviewing general-practice doctors about their use of prescription drugs. This proved to be a fascinating project during which I learned much about individual drugs and their application in primary healthcare.

After completion of the work placement, I worked as a window dresser in a department store in Canterbury, which proved to be enormous fun. Of course, I had no qualifications for the job other than my innate creativity! It transpired later that my boss had no qualifications either; he had made a fraudulent application and somehow got the job. During this time, I took out a girl called Kate, who worked in the cosmetics department, much to the chagrin of her boyfriend whom she married shortly afterwards.

My second work placement proved to be a remarkable experience. I came across an advertisement in one of the Sunday newspapers and applied for a position as a counsellor with Camp America, an organization which recruited young people to work in a wide variety of roles in North American summer camps for children. I discussed the idea with my parents, who were fully supportive. This was a marvellous opportunity to gain work experience in a foreign environment and also travel. My tutor also approved.

In the application form, we had to tick all those areas where we felt we had expertise and could contribute to summer-camp activities. I was probably a little over-zealous in my selections. When I received the offer of a position in Camp Zakelo, a summer camp in Maine, the northernmost state in the north-east of the United States, I had been assigned to teaching archery. I think I had probably shot a couple of arrows at Marlborough but that was about the sum of my archery expertise. In a panic, I hastily joined an archery club in Canterbury and attended a few sessions, claiming that I was very keen to learn archery. In the event, my job involved more supervision than teaching, so I got away with it.

I flew to Boston on 18th June 1970, the day of the general election that resulted in a surprise victory for the Conservative Party under leader Edward Heath. The Representation of the People Act

1969 lowered the voting age from twenty-one to eighteen, meaning that I was able to vote for the first time. However, I don't believe I did actually vote as I was on my way to the airport – before the days of postal voting.

My parents drove me to Heathrow Airport and we said an emotional goodbye; I would be gone for three months. This was my first grown-up trip abroad and my first time in an aeroplane, accompanied by a number of other Camp America recruits. There was a bad storm in mid-Atlantic with severe turbulence, which caused me some alarm and which happily I have never experienced since, other than in small aircraft in the tropics. We stayed a night or two in Boston before we all set off on our separate ways to camps in the region. I was the only counsellor heading for Camp Zakelo.

Camp Zakelo was set in beautiful grounds on the shores of Long Lake near Harrison, Maine, and was for wealthy Jewish boys as was evident from the camp's first-class facilities, a wide range of activities and excellent cooking. We lived in timber cabins – about a dozen boys and two counsellors in each. I was assigned to Cabin 11 with a co-counsellor called Winston (I don't recall his family name). I don't think we received any pay, other than perhaps some pocket money, but full board and expenses were provided as well as return flights from the UK.

I spent nine glorious weeks at Camp Zakelo and, of course, my duties extended well beyond archery. We sailed on the lake, climbed Mount Washington in New Hampshire, visited all sorts of interesting sites and led overnight camping trips to Sebago Lake State Park, where at least one counsellor would have to remain on duty all night. I used to enjoy sipping hot cocoa during the balmy summer nights.

On rare days off, I explored the region with other counsellors who had cars and were kind enough to take me out. We visited Casco Bay, where I went shark fishing, Reid State Park and Acadia National

Park, which has some stunning scenery and is just two hours' drive from the Canadian border.

There is no doubt that, as an Englishman, I was well received. I was living and working amongst an all-American cast. I loved it. My co-counsellors were incredibly friendly and we all got along well. On the whole, the boys behaved well, but there were times when my patience was tried, but I knew that patience was required. These advantaged boys would have no hesitation in encouraging their parents to sue for any misdemeanour. Upsetting wealthy Jewish parents in America was not to be recommended!

I was sad to leave Zakelo, one of the most memorable times of my life. I was probably a little homesick but I remember writing animated letters to my parents about my experiences, the people I met and their extraordinary hospitality. (Sadly, I no longer have the letters, although I retained them for years following the death of my father.) It was a completely new adventure, which I embraced enthusiastically.

One of my co-counsellors invited me to stay with his family (the Bennetts) on the Georgian Bay in Ontario, Canada, and we drove westwards in a classic Ford Mustang, staying in Niagara Falls en route. Sunset over the Georgian Bay was a lovely sight.

After that, I stayed with old family friends, the Underwood Grahams, who lived in Scientists' Cliffs, an upmarket district overlooking Chesapeake Bay, south of Washington DC. The husband – or Undy as he was known – was apparently a distant relative and worked in Government Communications Headquarters (GCHQ) in Cheltenham before retiring back home in the States. He never spoke about his work but we always assumed he was some sort of spy attached to the CIA.

I completed my trip in the USA visiting, once again, the Bennetts, with whom I had stayed on the Georgian Bay, in their luxury apartment on the Upper East Side of New York. They were all very good to me. The following year, they visited Canterbury and took me out for a very expensive meal.

Back to reality and textbooks for my third year at Brunel, during which I lived in lodgings in Hillingdon – much nearer The Red Lion! Much of our degree course was based on continuous assessment and I therefore devoted my time to delivering good-quality work and writing up my US work-placement experience.

My last work placement, in 1971, was based in Turku, the old capital of Finland. I stayed with a family, the Mikkonens, the arrangement being that I would teach the children, Isto and Johanna, English while I wrote my degree thesis. Valde Mikkonen, the husband, was a lecturer at Turku University and he was effectively my tutor for this project: *The Development of Diagnostic Language Tests for Prospective Finnish Medical Students*. The connection of this thesis with my degree course in psychology may appear a little flimsy, but I was designing tests which required an understanding of research techniques and the interpretation of data, both of which form an important part of any psychology course.

This was rather a lonely period. I spent much of my time working on my own, only meeting the family at meal times (supposedly for English lessons) or for the evening sauna. In the afternoons, I would often walk in the nearby forest where I sometimes came across Valde's wife, Ella, who had clearly taken a shine to me.

It was another fascinating three months of my life. I enjoyed working on the dissertation but we had fun too. Valde and Ella took me to parties, where the Finns often drank medicinal alcohol. I also travelled in Finland, including a trip to Rovaniemi, from where I crossed the Arctic Circle. I stayed up most of the night in broad daylight.

My last year at Brunel was spent living in a hall of residence, which was infinitely preferable to my first-year lodgings in Gerrards Cross, sharing a flat with Chris Bell in Bayswater in our second year, and digs in year three. The hall of residence provided a proper base, on campus, with fellow students all around and an altogether more manageable environment. I enjoyed this time, even though we had to sit exams during our last summer term.

On 15th July 1972, I graduated with an honours degree (upper-second class) in psychology. My parents attended graduation day, which was one of the hottest in July, and my father complained for months that he had been deprived of sitting in the garden on the best day of summer. There were no grand celebrations. The three of us had dinner at a Berni Inn in Canterbury; for me, almost certainly prawn cocktail, fillet steak and ice cream – still my favourites. Christopher could not attend, presumably because he was working.

At some point during my university days, I met a Swedish girl, Kerstin, at a party in London. We hit it off immediately and enjoyed many more parties together, one with my best friend, Robert, whose flat had a small rooftop. Kerstin decided to climb onto the roof but unfortunately slipped and broke her leg. We had probably all had far too much to drink.

We kept in touch for many years. Kerstin visited England in 1974. I picked her up at Heathrow Airport and we made the rather tedious journey to see my parents in Charing, where they had moved in 1973. We arrived at about 4.00 pm and I offered her a cup of tea or coffee. She replied, 'Gin and tonic, please.' My parents and I were a little taken aback as drinks were not generally served until 6.00 pm. So we started on the G&Ts. We returned to my flat in Belsize Park in London two days later and then set off for a highly successful tour of Scotland. Thereafter, I visited Sweden and Finland on several occasions.

I was very taken by Sweden, having visited Kerstin in Stockholm during my work placement in Finland. So, following my graduation, I arranged to drive to Sweden with my parents and Aunty Mary (one of my father's two elder sisters). The plan was to stay in Stockholm with my godfather, Philip Sprent, and his wife, Lois. Aunty Mary volunteered her car, a Singer Vogue, as it was a little larger and newer than my father's Singer Gazelle.

I had worked out the whole itinerary to the last detail. Having risen at some ungodly hour, we set off from Canterbury shortly after dawn. Father drove first; I took the wheel in Calais. We spent the first night in Bremen in north Germany and the second on a yacht hotel in Copenhagen before arriving in Stockholm on the third day – exactly on time!

We had an exceptional time in this beautiful city, rightly known as the Jewel of the Baltic or the Venice of the North. The Sprents were very good to us. They insisted on taking us to one of the famous palaces, Drottningholm Palace, where we spent a full day, which was far too long in my book. My heart sank when they suggested returning the following day to complete the tour. They also invited Kerstin to dinner when we had steak which had not been fully defrosted.

We went home via Gothenburg, on the west coast, where my father managed to drive the wrong way up a one-way street, much to the amusement of the pedestrians, before we embarked on the overnight boat which took us to Immingham in Lincolnshire. We all drank several Carlsbergs from rather stumpy bottles. Later, Aunty Mary complained that she felt very woozy.

If I am honest, I did not really enjoy my time at Brunel. The academic component I found stimulating, which motivated me to work hard, and I relished the summer work placements. But, although I fared well and had a few good friends, I never really felt that I fitted in. Oxbridge, rather than Uxbridge, would have been more my cup of tea! Nor did I enjoy my years at St George's School and Marlborough College. I had no grumbles about learning – far from it – but I found it difficult to live in these environments, particularly at school where the lack of privacy impinged upon me. I was never one of the 'boys' who enjoyed communal life, sports and the rough and tumble of everyday male living.

Nonetheless, with hindsight, I have surprised myself. Looking back, I realize how very fortunate I was and what a wonderful education I had. I was indeed privileged. This is especially true of Marlborough, which I regard as a first-class educational institution, which is why I keep in touch and accept invitations to various events at the college, cocktail parties in London and Hong Kong, and even fund-raising lunches. When my wife and I were looking at schools for my daughter, Sarah, we looked at Marlborough. However, for various reasons – astronomical fees aside – we decided it was not right for her and sent her to Wells Cathedral School. This was a very good decision; she loved it.

During my university years, I was preoccupied with my future, particularly my career. Medicine was not to be, and I am not sure that I had any real regrets. In retrospect, I wonder if I could ever have been a doctor in today's world. I loved psychology and was interested in moving on to a higher degree, specializing in clinical psychology. In fact, I was offered a place on a master's course in clinical psychology at Birmingham University but, unfortunately, finance was not available. My parents could not afford to keep me (I had a grant for my first degree) and I did not feel that I could finance the course myself. Sadly, I turned down the offer.

I sometimes wonder, had I been able to pursue this course, what my future would have held – certainly very different from how it turned out. I also think, in retrospect, that it may not have been right for me. I believe that I would have enjoyed the life of an academic, teaching psychology at university, but not as a clinical psychologist.

My parents were honestly not very helpful; they understood medicine, the law and the church. Any mention of advertising, finance or insurance, the choice of so many of my friends who were not committed to a 'profession', was met with horror. So, although I was at liberty to do as I wished, I sometimes felt that I was expected to pursue a professional career.

I thought very seriously about joining the Royal Navy – perhaps because my father was in the navy during the Second World War and I love the sea and ships, and of course the opportunity for travel, which was always close to my heart. My issue was privacy. Could I cope with living in restricted quarters with little privacy? If you have ever seen the officers' quarters on a modern destroyer, you will understand my concern. Although my father was all in favour and encouraged me, the navy became a bit of a joke because I would regularly ask for the application forms – I'm not sure I ever filled them in – and finally I received a reply telling me that I was too old to apply. That was the end of the navy.

I was also very interested in the Diplomatic Service – or Foreign Office as it is more properly known. A career in the Foreign Office provided the perfect opportunity for travel and working in an administrative role – in the widest sense – with security and a good pension. There were three stages to the application and I don't think I progressed beyond the first. I was disappointed. The fact was that, under Harold Wilson's Labour Government at the time, I had no hope of acceptance. Successful candidates were generally selected from grammar or secondary-modern schools. I was a public-school boy and we were *persona non grata*. I have friends recently retired from the Foreign Office on enormous pensions – all from grammar schools.

My friend Robert's father, Sir Robert Atkinson, had a significant influence on my life. He was a very successful businessman and had a strong character – traits that were perhaps lacking in my own father. He insisted that Robert should become an accountant and he suggested that I should do the same, pointing out that, with an accountancy qualification, you could work in any industry. In September 1972, Robert reluctantly joined Cooper Brothers, merged into PricewaterhouseCoopers more than twenty years ago. He hated it.

Coopers was based in Gutter Lane in the City of London. The story goes that the partners of Coopers wrote to the City of London Council, suggesting that they change the name of the road to Coopers Lane. After all, Coopers was probably the number-one accountancy firm in the world at that time. Apparently, after due consideration by members of the council, a reply was received, suggesting that the partners change the name of the firm to Gutter Brothers. I believe that was the end of the matter. Gutter Lane exists to this day and is unique as it is the only street with this name in Great Britain.

At about the same time, I was offered a position as an articled clerk with a leading accountancy firm, Peat, Marwick, Mitchell & Co (now KPMG), in Ironmonger Lane in the City. I was so proud to receive a beautifully written letter from the senior partner but, after much thought, I turned down the offer. I was much more interested in the property field as I felt that it embraced the built environment and one could be involved in urban planning, property development and many other facets of everyday living that were closer to real life than crunching numbers.

Chapter 5
The City

1972-1984

Sir Robert Atkinson once again came to the fore and introduced me to Kenneth Easter, a senior partner in Jones Lang Wootton (usually referred to as JLW), situated at 33 King Street in the City of London. At the time, Sir Robert was chairman of an engineering company, a client of JLW. And so it was that I embarked upon a career in property. I joined JLW in September 1972 at an annual salary of £1,001 (I have never understood the one).*

I was assigned to the Industrial Department of JLW and I am not sure that my immediate boss, Lance Slater, knew what to do with me. But I quickly found my way and was soon transferred to the valuation section where I excelled as a valuer of industrial property.

While working, I was studying in the evenings and at weekends to qualify as a chartered surveyor. Since I was a graduate – albeit not of estate management – I was able to follow an accelerated course of

---

* *The position would command a salary in the region of £25-30,000 today.*

study and finally received my diploma as an Associate of the Royal Institution of Chartered Surveyors in 1974. The ceremony, which my mother and brother attended, took place at the institution's elegant and historic headquarters in Great George Street, a stone's throw from the Palace of Westminster. I became a Fellow in the 1990s and remain a retired member to this day.

I was very good at what I did but I am not quite sure I understood the point of it all. I was sent off with an experienced colleague – more often than not catching a 7.30 am train from King's Cross or Euston to head northwards – to inspect factories and warehouses and assess the value of the property (having regard to the business operations too). I travelled throughout Britain and was fascinated by 'industry' – dark satanic mills in Yorkshire, turkey farms in Norfolk, fish-processing factories in Lincolnshire, and every possible variety of British manufacturing you can imagine.

In those days, we had to wear a suit and tie, with conventional leather shoes, notwithstanding that we might be exploring every nook and cranny of some Victorian factory or a building site with construction in full swing – perhaps in the heat of summer or in pouring rain. The only consolation was that JLW generously gave us a shoe allowance, which enabled those of us who looked after our shoes carefully to build up quite a stock of good-quality shoes – perhaps not comparable to Imelda Marcos but nonetheless a valuable perk. Nobody ever believed that we actually received a shoe allowance, and I have never heard of any other employer providing such a perk.

In those days, business expenses were quite generous. We would usually have breakfast on the train – silver service in First Class was available to all passengers, albeit we travelled in Second Class – and rent a car to get us around the various properties we needed to inspect. We stayed in fine hotels, usually selected by me from Egon Ronay's guides to hotels and restaurants, enjoying a couple of whiskies before dinner, a fillet steak and some good red wine – all in moderation, of course.

It seems to be a theme in my life but I am not sure I was particularly happy or fulfilled in my career at this stage. I once said to my boss, Kenneth Easter, that what I really wanted was to be a photographer. He advised me wisely: 'You need to stick with your day job; keep photography as a hobby.' He was probably right.

I did well and, after two or three years, was sent off on my own with junior staff, with responsibility for turning in full reports for clients. The reports were signed off by Kenneth but I believe he had complete trust in my judgement, although we would always discuss the figures included in the reports. After all, as a partner, he was ultimately responsible.

On one occasion, I volunteered to go to Sweden to value a factory. This enabled me to see Kerstin while I was there. The problem was that we went to a party on Midsummer's Eve and drank vast quantities of Swedish schnapps. I met Kenneth the following morning to drive him to the factory – not feeling my best.

During my first year at JLW, I shared a flat with a divorced teacher at 61 Eccleston Square in Pimlico. He lived in a complete shambles and disappeared every weekend, which was a great relief to me. I remember one night coming out of my bedroom to find flames leaping out of an oil-filled frying pan left on the hob. I have no recollection of how I extinguished the fire but happily no harm was done. Nonetheless, it was a very convenient arrangement since I could walk to Victoria Station and take the Tube to Mansion House and be in the office in about forty minutes.

There was a wonderful sense of camaraderie in JLW and my colleagues and I would often go for a beer after work in one of the nearby pubs. If we stayed too long, it was easy enough for me to stagger to the Tube and be back home for supper very quickly. On Friday evenings, a group of us used to go to the Coach & Horses in Hill Street, just off Berkeley Square, where property professionals from many firms would meet.

I lost touch with most of my colleagues after leaving JLW, but met many of them again in April 2018 when I attended the funeral of Dick Harvey, a colleague with whom I worked very closely. He sat opposite me in the office, puffing away at his pipe. I well remember us working by gaslight during the three-day week, introduced by Edward Heath's government on 1st January 1974 to avoid a standstill of British industry resulting from the oil crisis in late 1973 and the threat of a strike by coal miners.

Since I was now earning, I also had my first grown-up holiday abroad (not including university summer work placements). I booked a half-board package holiday, for me alone, to Arenal in Majorca. It was probably for four or five nights and cost about £26. It was springtime in England with a chill in the air. I rushed off to Austin Reed in Regent's Street on the morning of my departure to buy a navy polo-neck sweater, which cost over £6 – quite expensive in those days.

The hotel was certainly not five-star but I had an amazing time. I have no recollection of how it came to happen but I met, or was introduced to, a wealthy lady called Mary Huggins, who lived in a huge house in the best area of the island and owned a Fiat sports car. Since she was quite elderly, she did not drive any more and rarely got out of the house, so she made me an offer I could not refuse: I would drive her around the island in exchange for lunch in a high-end restaurant every day. She was happy to have my company and get out and about; I was able to see the whole island in comfort and enjoy some very good food and wine. We covered a good part of the island but focused on the north-west coast, which is very beautiful.

It was this wonderful and generous lady who introduced me to her old friend, Canon Willy Passmore, who was staying in Majorca and was the priest-in-charge of the Anglican church in Alassio in north-west Italy. As a result of this introduction and follow-up by my father, my parents and I, sometimes with friends and relations, enjoyed two holidays in Alassio.

*

In 1973, my father was instituted as Vicar and Rector, Charing with Charing Heath and Little Chart in Kent. The vicarage was a beautiful fourteenth-century building but had no central heating, a decaying kitchen and was in need of total redecoration, so they remained in the house in Canterbury while the vicarage was renovated. Father held the unusual post of non-resident Vicar of Charing and Rector of Little Chart until August 1974 when my parents moved into the vicarage. During this interim period, my father's parish office was a caravan wired up to the nearby church barn, with all mod cons.

After a little over a year in Eccleston Square, I moved to Haverstock Hill in Belsize Park in 1974, where I shared a flat with Susan Cooper. We did not know each other when we met to discuss the flat but became very good friends. We lived separate lives but I would often join her for dinner and we once went to Paris together to join some of her friends. We still keep in touch, although a meeting is long overdue.

I think she had some idea that I might be gay – perhaps because I was not living with a woman and did not appear to have girlfriends. Later that year, Kerstin came to stay in the flat and I believe I was vindicated.

In the spring, Robert and I decided to tour the Loire Valley in France in his Mini. We enjoyed ourselves immensely, eating freshly prepared food from inexpensive *prix fixe* menus in small country bistros, sipping Sancerre and Anjou wines with a picnic and exploring the historic quarters of Tours, the principal city of the Loire Valley.

Finding accommodation, which we had not pre-booked, proved a challenge.

'*Est-ce que vous avez deux chambres pour ce soir, s'il vous plaît?*' I would enquire of the proprietor of a nearby auberge every evening.

'*Non, nous sommes complets ce soir.*'

And so it went on. Somehow, we always managed to find somewhere to stay but I began to wonder about the French and their apparent Anglophobia. Perhaps it came about because we burned Joan of Arc at the stake or for our supposed crimes against perfectly good food. I was reminded of my hitch-hiking experience a few years earlier.

On our way home, the Mini's windscreen shattered in the village of Mamers, a good four hours' drive from Calais where our ferry was scheduled to depart at 7.00 pm. It was lunchtime. By some miracle, we found a small vehicle-repair shop which had a Mini windscreen in stock. The mechanics could not have been more helpful and the replacement windscreen was fitted by 2.00 pm. We exceeded all speed limits on the way to Calais, arriving just in time to board. It was a close shave.

A year later, I was very fortunate in being able to move into Dolphin Square, a block of some 1,250 flats on the river in Pimlico, built in the mid-1930s. At the time, it was sometimes described as 'the largest self-contained block of flats in Europe'. As a housing association administered by the Dolphin Square Trust, a sub-lessee of Westminster City Council, the flats were only available to rent – at very attractive rentals, it has to be said.

Although I did not technically qualify for residency as I did not work in the City of Westminster, the general manager allowed me to take over the flat previously rented by my brother, Christopher, who was moving into a larger flat in Dolphin Square. The flat was a large studio on the sixth floor of Raleigh House, overlooking the square's beautiful gardens and bathed in north light. There was a swimming pool too, which I used most mornings before work. I spent a good deal of time and money furnishing this lovely studio, my first real home, and I had a lot of fun here, entertaining a number of girlfriends as well as family and friends.

My parents did not have the easiest of relationships. On one occasion, my father telephoned me at short notice and came to visit me for the day to enjoy some respite from the trying situation at home. While he was with me, my mother telephoned in rather a state. 'Hello, darling. Your father's gone off somewhere and I've no idea where. I'm so worried. Has he been in touch with you?'

'He's here with me,' I confessed.

I am not sure what happened after that but I knew I had to give an honest answer. I think Father spoke to my mother and everything appeared to be fine.

During the day, my father told me they had decided to buy another dog, not having owned a dog since Marcus in the early Windsor days. He was a puppy, a Welsh border collie, which he named Abel. He proved to be a wonderful companion for fourteen years.

We also plotted a West Country tour for the two of us for a few days later in the month, which took us as far west as Flushing in Cornwall. We stayed a night with Susan, my 'landlady' in Haverstock Hill, who was attending Falmouth School of Art, and enjoyed a meal at an excellent but inexpensive fish restaurant – perhaps best described as a shack – on the quayside. In those days, Flushing had its own little fleet of oyster smacks and the fishermen's cottages could be bought for a song.

I enjoyed two happy years in Dolphin Square and rather sadly left in 1977 to move into my first owned property.

In 1976, a temp employee appeared in the office. Her name was Elaine Clay. She had returned from Durban in South Africa, where she had been working, because she felt it was time to come home. I think she fondly imagined that she might return to South Africa at some point but there were no plans in place. In the event, Elaine and I started going out together and we became involved. In the late summer, we stayed with her sister, Ann, and her husband, Stephen, who owned a farm in Yockleton, a small village seven miles west of Shrewsbury.

I think that Kenneth Easter was very heedful of our relationship. He was perceptive and cared a lot about his staff. He spent a good deal of time talking to Elaine outside office hours. Elaine told me just recently, when I asked her to review this section of my manuscript, that Kenneth fancied her and simply wanted to have an excuse to spend time with her. I had no idea about this apparent mild infatuation and was somewhat amused to hear of it more than forty years later. Regardless of Kenneth's motives, I believe he was also sensitive to some unresolved issues emanating from her somewhat challenging childhood.

The following year, Elaine and I bought a one-bedroom flat together in Harrowdene Gardens, Teddington, for about £13,500.* This was the most we could afford, with a mortgage, and I had to persuade my father to ask Lloyds Bank, administrator of my grandmother's trust, if the trustees would allow me to draw down a small advance for the deposit. (The trust would not normally have matured until my father's death and it provided him with a very small income.) The bank agreed on the basis that it was a sensible investment, which proved to be the case, and was certainly preferable to the bank's rather uninspired investment choices. Christopher followed with a similar request, which was of course granted.

Elaine and I sent out cards telling people of our exciting news. I forget whether Donald Fehrenbach, my father's colleague from Windsor days, wrote to me or if he simply cut us off but he certainly did not approve of our living together in an unmarried state! I don't believe I ever saw him again.

In 1977, I was offered the position of valuation surveyor at Imperial Foods Ltd, part of the giant Imperial Group plc of tobacco fame.

---

*   *In today's market, the property would be worth in excess of £300,000.*

I was sad to leave JLW but felt that my prospects were limited in the short term, and there is little doubt that I was attracted by the much higher salary, company car and other perks.

The following year, I was offered a job with a property firm in Malawi, East Africa. Although I had not been with Imperial Foods for long, I was still keen to work overseas. Elaine and I had several meetings with the partners in London and all the arrangements were set up. We met Kenneth for a drink to ask him if he would provide a reference.

'Kenneth, I've been offered a job in Malawi and I'd like you to be a referee,' I said.

'What sort of job?'

'Well, it's basically to run the valuation and professional side of a London-based firm which has an office in Malawi. It's a marvellous opportunity for us and we are keen to work overseas.'

Kenneth mulled over my words and eventually said, 'I don't believe that this move would be right for you. I'm sorry but I would not be comfortable giving you a reference.'

We were both taken aback and went our separate ways. I had other references so his unwillingness to agree did not actually matter. Kenneth always came straight to the point and, in the event, he was right.

We both needed visas, of course. However, it transpired that Elaine would not be able to obtain the visa required to come with me other than as my wife.

'It looks like we're going to have to get married,' I said after visiting the Malawi High Commission.

As Elaine told me when she was reminding me of the sequence of events, it was not the most romantic proposal a girl could hope for, but it was obviously the spur we needed to plan our wedding.

With the visa issue resolved, I wrote a letter of resignation from Imperial Foods and left it in my boss's secretary's in tray. By some miracle, I received a message the very same evening from my prospective employers saying that they would have to withdraw their offer because of some new government hurdle which would make it impossible for me to take up the position. I was able to return to the secretary's office under cover of darkness and hastily remove my letter. Fate was on my side and, of course, nobody was ever the wiser. Elaine and I were very disappointed but it was certainly for the best.

This all happened about six weeks before our wedding but, having come so far with all the arrangements, we decided to go ahead as planned. And so, on 6th May 1978, we were married in Ashford Registry Office. Our witnesses were Christopher and Elaine's sister, Ann. We were not permitted to marry in church because Elaine had been divorced. My father implored the bishop to make an exception but in those days the rules governing the marriage of divorcees in church were less flexible than they are today. Following the civil ceremony, there was a blessing, conducted by my father, in Charing Church and a gathering of family and friends in the vicarage.

Elaine and I departed later in the afternoon to spend a few nights away. We had not planned a honeymoon because we assumed that we would be departing for Malawi shortly after our wedding. However, I was keen to take Elaine to Scotland, which I loved so much, and we enjoyed a week in the early summer touring the West Coast and the Highlands. Among many of my favourite places, we visited Newtonmore – close to the geographical centre of Scotland – where my three great aunts used to live. I have so many childhood memories of walking on the moors by the River Calder, which skirts the village and has always been a special place for me. I took Elaine there and we lay on the riverbank listening to the burbling of the shallow water as it ran over the rocks.

Since the Malawi plan had fallen apart, we decided to spend a week or two on a belated honeymoon on the Greek island of Spetses. It was September, with temperatures of around twenty-five degrees Celsius and glorious dry, sunny days.

Unfortunately, the night before we flew to Greece, Elaine cut her head open on the open door of a kitchen cupboard. I took her to Kingston Hospital where she received several stitches. The nurse then informed me that they would need to be removed before we were back from Spetses; I would therefore have to perform the task. I panicked but somehow managed to complete the operation.

Elaine and I also spent two holidays with my parents. In 1977, we drove to Alassio, where my father was covering for Willy Passmore, the incumbent of the Anglican church, while he was on holiday. I grew a beard while we were there. Two years later, the four of us went to a chalet, which belonged to a friend of Elaine, high up in the hills of Austria. Elaine and my parents got on very well and both holidays were a great success.

At some point during this period, I was offered a job as a lecturer at the Polytechnic of the South Bank – now London South Bank University. I had always been attracted by the idea of a career in academia and the head of the Valuation Department, John Ratcliffe, encouraged me to apply. I was called to an interview and was surprised to be seated in front of a panel of about six senior staff who interviewed me before asking me to wait outside. Shortly afterwards, I was called back.

The convener of the panel said, 'Mr Nourse, thank you for attending the interview. We have carefully considered your application and suitability for the post and would like to offer you a position as a lecturer in the Valuation Department.'

I was surprised that an offer was made there and then. I was expecting a letter to arrive in due course, advising me of the outcome of my interview, as would normally be the case in the business world.

'Thank you very much for your offer. I am grateful and very excited at the prospect of working with you. However, I do need time

81

to consider your offer and discuss it with my wife.'

'That would be most unusual with appointments in education,' replied the convener. 'You should really know that you're expected to accept or reject the offer immediately.'

I had no knowledge of how educational appointments were made and did not realize that one was expected to make a decision on the spot. I was completely nonplussed and did not know how to react.

'I'm sorry. I simply had no idea but I'm not in a position to give you an immediate answer. Would you please give me some time to consider the offer and discuss it with my wife?'

After conferring with other members of the panel, the convener said, 'All right. This is highly unusual but we will make an exception on this occasion and give you twenty-four hours to revert to us with your answer.'

'I am so grateful. Thank you, and my apologies for creating a precedent.'

I was torn. Here was a wonderful opportunity to pursue an academic career but it would mean significant changes to our lives. The salary was, of course, much lower than I was being paid by Imperial Foods and I would lose my company car and other perks. We had a mortgage and both Elaine and I were concerned about the financial implications. Reluctantly, I declined. John Ratcliffe was not very happy with me. I will never know whether this could have been a good move; it may, perhaps, have been the answer to all my ongoing doubts about the commercial property world which I had chosen to join.

The head office of Imperial Foods was based in a beautiful period building in Lygon Place, Victoria. My position as valuation surveyor was a senior one and, during my time with the company, I travelled the length and breadth of Britain as I undertook valuations of Imperial

Foods' properties. Subsidiaries included Ross Foods, Young's Seafood, Golden Wonder, Buxted Poultry and other household names, most of them still well-known brands today.

In 1979, Michael Davies, chairman of the company, called me into his vast pale-green office on the first floor. 'Sit down, Philip,' he said, gesturing me towards an armchair. He called for coffee and joined me in the chair opposite. 'Paul Draper has talked to me about moving away from the property side of the business and taking up a commercial role in the group. I'd like you to take over his position as group surveyor. I have complete faith in you and believe that you'll do an excellent job.'

Somewhat taken aback, I replied, 'Yes, of course. I would be privileged. What's Paul going to do?'

'Well, we're fine-tuning his position now but he'll be involved in looking at strategies for the various businesses going forward.'

My new position would give me overall responsibility for the Property Division and management of a mixed portfolio of 2,000 properties. I was also appointed a director of the group's property-development subsidiary.

'By the way,' added Michael, 'there is one condition attached to my offer: you remove that beard of yours.' Like many employers, he disliked beards, believing that they do not give a clean and professional impression.

'That will not be a problem, Michael, I assure you.'

I quickly acquiesced but kept my moustache, which I removed on April Fool's Day 1994. Michael was happy; I was happy. I moved into a large, private office with a speakerphone, the ultimate status symbol in those days. I now qualified for drinks and lunch in the directors' dining room, which was always fun. My appointment as group surveyor caused some upset since one of my longer-serving colleagues had been passed over and would now report to me. In the event, he took over the position from me when I left the company.

*

Also that same year, 1979, Elaine and I moved to a duplex in Broom Close, Teddington, a development with lovely gardens running down to the River Thames, where I kept a small dinghy. It was here that Elaine's adoptive father, Anthony, told me to stop worrying about buying sofas and get on with producing a child! And so we did. Sarah Helen Nourse was born at 10.28 on the morning of 16th September 1980 in Kingston Hospital. I drove home after the birth and poured myself a very large whisky in celebration. At some later stage, I said that I was not very moved by the process of childbirth, for which I don't think I was ever quite forgiven.

I have so many memories of Sarah as a baby. Elaine would feed her and one of us would hold her over our shoulder, pacing up and down and patting her back to wind her. I think she was quite a good sleeper, but Elaine would have to get up to feed her in the night. I also comforted her at night sometimes if she was crying or in some way distressed. I used to take Sarah out for walks in her pushchair, not feeling entirely confident in myself, but at least giving Elaine a short break from the relentless duties of motherhood.

Not long after Sarah was born, my Uncle Peter, my father's eldest brother, having learned that Elaine had given birth to a daughter, wrote me a long and serious letter urging me to exercise my family duty and ensure the continuity of the Nourse name, I being the only member of the family who was likely to father a son. His letter caused us much mirth but sadly his exhortation was never fulfilled.

One of my last memories of Broom Close was the wedding of Prince Charles and Lady Diana Spencer on 29th July 1981 in St Paul's Cathedral. Elaine and I entertained our good friend Robert and his wife, Lynn, and we all sat glued to the television while drinking champagne to celebrate the couple's marriage. Billed as a fairy-tale wedding, the marriage was watched by an estimated television audience of 750 million. It was a remarkable day, with crowds lining the route of Diana's procession, waving flags and lapping up the pomp and ceremony of the occasion.

In September, we set off with Sarah to Seaton, my parents' holiday home in Devon. Sarah was now almost one year old and I think Elaine was exhausted. A day or two later, she asked Ann, her sister, if she would look after Sarah for a few days. We made the four-hour drive to her home in Yockleton, returning to Seaton where we enjoyed a few days of respite.

Not long afterwards, Elaine and I moved to an Edwardian terraced house at 29 Teddington Park Road. It was an elegant house with a large kitchen, where we had an old pine table and dresser, a combined living/dining room, three bedrooms and a garden. We spent many weeks renovating this house.

We enjoyed some happy times in Teddington with many friends coming to see us, including Annie and John (no longer with us), Dan and Sarah, our next-door neighbours, and Susan, whom Elaine met at Reliance, an employment agency in Kingston upon Thames. Susan visited us often and turned out to be a brick, often babysitting for us. The three of us used to drink far too much, of course, and we would play Dionne Warwick's 'Heartbreaker' (written by the Bee Gees) at full volume.

Christopher's Brazilian partner, Mario, whom we both adored, came to lunch in our lovely pinewood kitchen one day. Unfortunately, we touched on the subject of the Falklands War, a conflict between Argentina and the United Kingdom, which led to a huge argument as Mario was a staunch supporter of Argentina. All was forgiven at some point, of course, and we remain good friends to this day, as I do with so many of these wonderful friends from the 1980s.

In late 1981, Elaine and I were having dinner in one of my favourite restaurants near Bushy Park when she announced, quite unexpectedly, that she no longer wished to be married to me. I was dumbfounded. We tried to work on our relationship, we went to marriage counsellors and a psychotherapist, and I moved out for a period of weeks. My father spent many hours counselling Elaine, helping her to understand what the next steps might look like and how best to manage them. He was very much the realist but I know that both he and my mother would like to have seen Elaine and me together again.

In April 1983, we separated. We had sold the house and divided the proceeds equally. Elaine bought a flat nearby in Stanley Road and I bought a flat in Kew Road, Richmond, overlooking the Old Deer Park and the Great Pagoda in Kew Gardens. When I parted company with her and Sarah at their new front door, I said, 'Go well, my friend, and love my daughter.' Terribly unhappy, I went to stay with my old friend from school, Malcolm Caithness.

We were formally divorced on 22nd May 1984 in Wandsworth County Court. A month before, we appeared at a child-custody hearing before His Honour Judge Hunter.

'Custody to the mother,' he announced as a matter of course.

'No, Your Honour, we agreed joint custody,' countered Elaine.

The judge, embarrassed, coughed and said, 'Yes, of course. Custody to the Petitioner and Respondent, with care and control to the Respondent.'

It was, by and large, an amicable arrangement, although there were some issues later, usually concerning maintenance payments for Sarah.

Elaine had been seeing a former Catholic priest, Martin, who lived in Strawberry Hill, during the last few months of our living together. I believe the relationship was probably good for her at this time and I am sure he offered pastoral care, although I suspect that he may have struggled with a sense of 'Catholic guilt'. I also started seeing a girl called Claire. I recall bringing her back a wood carving from Bali in Indonesia, which I had recently visited, but I remember little else about this brief relationship.

I loved my flat in Richmond. I was very sad and lonely, but I somehow managed to begin a new life. My downstairs neighbour, Mrs Elsey, who must have been in her late sixties, was incredibly good to me. She insisted on doing my ironing. Every Monday evening, I used to visit her flat to pick up my shirts and she would ply me with vast quantities of whisky and ginger ale.

'Will it be your usual, dear?'

'That would be lovely, thank you. You are very good to me, Mrs E.'

'It's my pleasure, dear. I'm on my own most of the time and I enjoy your company.'

And she would plod off to the kitchen to pour me the first of several very healthy measures of Scotch.

We were usually glued to the television, watching Jayne Torvill and Christopher Dean, who won Gold for skating to Ravel's *Boléro* at the Sarajevo Olympics in 1984 (watched by a British television audience of more than twenty-four million). I would then stagger up the stairs to my own flat for a simple Monday supper.

At this time, I began dating a girl called Chrissie, who was very supportive. I had met her at a party shortly before Elaine and I separated.

We were chatting and I said, 'Would you like to come out for a drink with me one day?'

'I don't go out with married men,' she said with some apparent disappointment.

But as soon as I was ensconced in my new flat in Richmond, we did go out. We were like chalk and cheese – in every respect – but we got on very well.

Sarah used to spend every other weekend (or at least one out of three) with me. I only had one bedroom so she slept on a folding bed which fitted neatly into the bay window. We often went for walks in Kew Gardens, two minutes' walk away, and met friends for lunch or in their homes. Sometimes, Sarah and I would go out with Chrissie and her six-year-old son, Jamie, who was very good with Sarah. When we got home, I would give her supper which, I am ashamed to admit, consisted more often than not of fish fingers and baked beans. She loved it.

Sarah was only two and a half when Elaine and I separated. I would have expected her to be showing all the symptoms of the 'terrible twos' and yet I have no recollection of defiant behaviour, temper tantrums and the like. I did not find it easy looking after her on my own but we had fun.

I enjoyed my job with Imperial Foods and, unlike working in professional practice, there was happily no pressure to earn fees. However, I missed the camaraderie that we all enjoyed at Jones Lang Wootton – and indeed in most professional firms. At 5.30 pm, most staff would go home, whereas at JLW we would work late and often repair to the pub.

One of the highlights was working with Bidwells, a Cambridge-based property consultancy specializing in rural and agricultural property. Tim Lawson, the senior partner, James Buxton, his assistant, and I used to fly to Scotland and visit farms owned by Imperial Foods, assessing their value and deciding how best we could dispose of those properties no longer required.

In 1982, most of the trading operations of Imperial Foods were sold to Hillsdown Holdings, which caused a huge upheaval. We had to move our head office – presumably on cost grounds – from Lygon Place in Victoria to an out-of-London location. After much research, Bedford was chosen as the most suitable location and, in 1983, we all moved to a brand-new office building. We were given the option of staying or leaving – with compensation.

By now, I was living in Richmond and I worked in the new office for a month or two to see how I would feel – staying in a hotel at the company's expense from Monday to Friday – before reaching the conclusion that Bedford was not for me. I decided to leave and received a generous severance package. I left some good friends in Imperial Foods, including Guy Curry, Jane Henry and Michael Barratt, who worked in the Legal Department, and Richard Gage and Peter Taylor, who worked alongside me. We still keep in touch from time to time.

During this period, I was interviewed by PA Consulting for a position with a major property developer in Jakarta, Indonesia, and in 1983 was flown there to meet the directors. I spent a couple of days with them and we even looked at some properties where I might live. I felt that I had a good chance of being offered the job but I never heard another word: not from the developer, not from PA Consulting. In those days, it was usual to receive a letter confirming whether or not one had been successful in a job application, although today it is commonplace not to receive any feedback at all. I concluded that it was a non-starter.

I was concerned about leaving Sarah but I think my preoccupation with moving overseas – running away, perhaps – eclipsed my feelings of paternal responsibility, and the guilt haunted me for many years to come.

Whilst in Jakarta, I was able to divert my flight home via Hong Kong where my close friend, Robert, was now working with Cathay Pacific Airways. He was actually employed as 'house staff' by the Swire Group in London and had been posted to Hong Kong. Before flying to Hong Kong, I made a short side trip to Bali, best known as a tropical paradise in the Indonesian archipelago. I stayed in a hotel in Sanur on the south-east coast. Ten years later, I was to return to Bali with my second wife and I am convinced we stayed in the same hotel – an extraordinary coincidence.

I then went to stay with Robert and this was my first introduction to Hong Kong. I followed the tourist route and Robert also took me to all sorts of places, including naughty bars in one of Hong Kong's nightlife districts.

'After we've eaten, I'll show you Wanchai,' Robert said. 'There are many girlie bars, frequented by American sailors as well as gweilos.'*

'Sounds good to me,' I replied with some hesitation. I was not sure what I was getting myself into.

'San Francisco Bar in Lockhart Road, please,' Robert instructed the taxi driver.

I must admit that I had never been into a place quite like this. On entering the bar through heavy tie-back curtains, I was confronted by a huge oval bar and numerous girls wandering around or chatting up customers. Most of the girls were attractive, sexily clad Filipinas or Thais, but there were Chinese girls too.

We ordered two beers and, within minutes, we were joined by two girls.

'You buy me drink?'

It was difficult to refuse and, of course, a little later we were presented with a large bill. I think the girls were actually drinking tea.

Later, we wandered along Lockhart Road with its myriad bars tempting unwary customers into their darkened inner sanctums. We stopped at one of the many *dai pai dongs* (open-air food stalls), which offer cheap, freshly cooked Chinese dishes and are characterized by their big gas burners, sizzling food and the clanking of woks. We sat on stools at a brightly coloured plastic table and ordered Tsing Tao beers and a bowl of noodles before heading home.

In my early days in Hong Kong, my friends and I frequently visited the bars in Wanchai, getting home rather late with our wallets feeling a little lighter than we would have wished.

Robert also took me to the Foreign Correspondents' Club, which had recently relocated into a beautiful colonial brick and

---

* *Usually translated as 'ghost' or 'devil man', a Cantonese slang term for Westerners.*

stucco building dating from 1913 – formerly used as a cold-storage warehouse for ice and dairy products. The FCC, as it is known, is an august press club with a long and rich journalistic heritage dating back to its founding in China in 1943. The FCC has one of the longest bars in East Asia. It is four-sided with around thirty high swivelling chairs, which regulars have been known to fall off from time to time. The bar was packed with journalists of all ages, representing newspapers, magazines, television channels and media from all over the world, as well as non-journalist associate members. I was overawed by the ambience and vibrancy of this club, which I later joined.

I used my few days in Hong Kong wisely, arranging meetings with a number of property consultancies and developers. The market was not in very good shape at the time so I was not successful in landing a job. However, Chris Palmer, the senior partner of Richard Ellis (now CBRE), asked me if I would be interested in setting up an office in Bangkok, which he and his partners had been discussing. I said that I would be. I knew it was a long shot but returned home to England with the exciting prospect once again of living and working overseas.

Having left Imperial Foods, I needed to find a job and, in 1983, I was also discussing a new position with Weatherall Green & Smith, a professional firm of chartered surveyors in Chancery Lane in the heart of London's Inns of Court and other legal entities. I was interviewed by Hugh Chatwin, an eccentric but highly erudite character who was the brother of famous author Bruce Chatwin. After numerous in-depth discussions and written submissions, which I later discovered he had 'marked', I was offered a job. I had heard nothing further from Richard Ellis and decided to accept the offer, starting in September 1983. After six years with Imperial Foods, where I was happy, I was nevertheless delighted to be out of the wilderness and back working in professional practice. It seemed that I was not meant to work abroad.

Hugh, my immediate boss, and I got on like a house on fire and there was never any rush to get to the office on time since he was invariably late. He used to drive to the office with a mug of coffee (a proper china mug) perched on the dashboard. We were setting up a new venture, which involved advising on the availability of capital allowances and arranging tax-related leasing finance for industrial enterprises. I don't think anybody in the firm ever understood what we were up to – and I am not sure that I did – but Hugh's credibility worked wonders and we actually made some money.

I believe that David Yorke, the partner in charge of the department and to whom Hugh and I ultimately reported, had other aspirations for me. He would sometimes ask me into his office and give me a traditional client job, unrelated to Hugh's initiative, with a view to encouraging me back into mainstream professional work. I don't think Hugh was very happy about this.

In the 1980s, client lunches, accompanied by generous amounts of wine, were very much the norm. At Weatherall's, we were fortunate to have in-house catering and Hugh and I used to arrange Friday lunches on a regular basis. We started at 12.30 pm with aperitifs and then enjoyed fine wines with our food. The mistake was the port that invariably followed. Often, our lunches did not finish until around 6.00 pm.

It was at Weatherall Green & Smith that I met my future wife, Diane. She worked as a research assistant in the Research Department under Brian Waldy, who remains a good friend to this day. I was being given a tour of Weatherall's various departments and, on passing through Research, I noticed a girl, probably in her early thirties, with shortish black hair and large grey eyes, on my left. We acknowledged each other and I moved on. Diane – or Di as she has always been known to most of us – told me many years later that she knew I would be the man she would marry from the moment she first set eyes on me. Praise indeed!

We met on a few occasions in the coming weeks, the most famous being the Christmas party when I suggested she should come up to my office where we sat together in a rather small armchair. Afterwards, I accompanied Di to her home in St John's Wood, apparently carrying a rocking horse I had bought Sarah for Christmas. My friend Susan, who was such a brick in Teddington days, was expecting me at her party that evening but I was running late. I telephoned her, at least twice, to ask how late I could arrive. I made it to the party but I don't think she was best pleased.

Di and I were very much at one with each other and enjoyed our time together. She invited me to a black-tie dinner with her friend, Annie, and husband, Marcus, the architectural editor of *Country Life*, at their house in Cambridge Street, Pimlico. Annie's mother apparently said, 'Gosh, he's jolly handsome, Di.' I was flattered, of course. I also hosted a house-warming party in my new flat in Richmond to which I invited Di. I think she was very happy to be my 'consort'. Some of us went for a curry after the party; it was a highly successful and entertaining evening.

The difficulty for me started when Chris Palmer, whom I met in Hong Kong a year earlier, telephoned me at about 5.00 one morning (1.00 pm in Hong Kong).

'Philip, this is Chris Palmer, Richard Ellis in Hong Kong. How are you?'

'I'm fine, thank you. How nice to hear from you.'

'Look, I know we discussed your setting up an office in Bangkok, but Bangkok is a non-starter, at least for the time being. Why don't you come to Hong Kong instead? We want to establish an Industrial Department and, with your background, I think you would fit the bill.'

I was flabbergasted. It was 5.00 in the morning and I was being offered a job in Hong Kong. I could not believe it. After all, it was many months since Chris and I had spoken.

'Chris, that sounds amazing – Hong Kong. I am so grateful. Should we discuss the terms, timing and so on?'

'Look, Philip, I hadn't realized it was so early in the morning for you – my apologies for calling at this ungodly hour – so let me write to you with a formal offer, setting out all the details of salary, housing allowance etc. We would like you here as soon as possible, however.'

I thanked Chris profusely and put down the phone. My mind was in a spin. I did not get back to sleep.

I somehow had to tell Di that I would be going to Hong Kong. I had booked a trip for us to Honfleur in Normandy, France, over Easter. However, Hong Kong was imminent and I knew I had to spend time with my parents in their new home in Charing before my departure. I took her to one of my favourite restaurants in Kew, Le Mange Tout. I was on edge and unsure of myself.

'Look, I'm not sure how to say this, but I've been offered a job in Hong Kong, which I've accepted.'

Di obviously didn't quite know what to say and sat opposite me looking extremely downcast.

'I'm sorry. You know I've always wanted to work overseas and I can't turn down this opportunity.'

Di was too upset to eat her steak, which I apparently devoured for her without batting an eyelid.

'What about our trip to Honfleur at Easter?' she asked.

'I'm afraid we will have to cancel it. I'm expected in Hong Kong in early June and time is very short. I need to see my parents and will have to spend time with them over Easter. I'm very sorry but it's important for me to see them.'

Our relationship had really come to an end. I left England for Hong Kong feeling very bad about how I had treated Di. I was sad but excited at the prospect of a new opportunity.

I have also always felt enormous guilt about leaving Sarah

behind at the age of three and a half. In retrospect, I realized it was not a good decision. Elaine married again not long after we were divorced but, even so, Sarah needed her real father, and I missed her too.

Chapter 6

Heading East

1984-1987

On Sunday 3rd June 1984, I touched down at Hong Kong International Airport, more commonly known as Kai Tak Airport, notorious for its tricky low-level approach over Kowloon, one of the densest urban areas in the world.

I was immediately struck by the noise, the seething mass of people and the unmistakable smells of Hong Kong. Signs in English and Chinese in every direction, the Cantonese shouting at one another, the sheer sense of energy: this was Hong Kong, a far cry from the relative lassitude of Richmond or even Weatherall Green & Smith and Chancery Lane.

I was met by Chris Palmer, who drove me to the Marco Polo Hotel (now the Gateway Hong Kong, I believe) in Canton Road, Tsimshatsui, where I was to stay while I settled in. I had never visited this part of the Kowloon Peninsula and, driving from the airport, I was astonished by the sheer density of buildings – old high-rise tenement blocks badly in need of renovation and factories all around.

It was hard to imagine how people lived in these conditions. Once we reached the heart of Tsimshatsui, a major commercial and tourist hub on the southern tip of Kowloon, the streets were teeming with people shopping, meeting friends or simply escaping the confines of their small apartments.

'How was your flight?' Chris asked.

'Very good, thank you. It's a long flight but the time seemed to pass quite quickly. I didn't really manage to sleep, though.'

'Let's go and have a beer or two and then I'll leave you to it,' Chris suggested as he parked the car. We went to the Tartan Bar and chatted for the best part of an hour.

'Tomorrow, we'll go to the dragon-boat races. The weather forecast is not good – torrential rain by the look of it – but we'll have fun. I'll pick you up about 10.30 if that's OK?'

'That sounds good. I look forward to it.'

I spent a restless night after the long flight. As planned, Chris met me and we drove through the Cross-Harbour Tunnel to Stanley, a small seafront village on the south side of Hong Kong Island.

The Dragon Boat Festival falls on the fifth day of the fifth month in the Chinese lunar calendar. The colourful festivities have their origins in a tragedy that supposedly occurred 2,000 years ago. The festival, also known as Tuen Ng Festival, commemorates the death of Qu Yuan, a Chinese national hero. In a protest against corrupt rulers, Qu drowned himself in the Mi Lo River. To scare away fish from eating his body, the townspeople beat drums and threw glutinous rice dumplings called *zongzi* into the water.

The real highlight of the festival is the fierce-looking dragon boats racing in a lively, colourful spectacle. Teams race the elaborately decorated boats to the beat of heavy drums. These special boats, which measure more than ten metres in length, have ornately carved and painted dragon heads and tails, and each boat carries a crew of around twenty paddlers.

It was indeed pouring with rain in Stanley and continued to do so for most of the day. I had no idea what to expect but was led onto a large junk, a typical Chinese flat-bottomed timber boat, moored in the harbour amongst hundreds of other boats, where I was introduced to numerous people, including Chris's wife, Sarah. This was my first day in Hong Kong; teeming rain, high humidity, copious amounts of alcohol and a very sociable crowd. We probably watched a good many dragon-boat races but I believe the main focus of the day was eating, drinking and socializing. I was somewhat awestruck.

The next day – feeling a little jaded – I took the Star Ferry across the harbour and walked to Richard Ellis's head office in Edinburgh Tower in Hong Kong's Central District. Here, I met the other partners, including Chris Thrift who was to be my boss in the Kowloon office. After this first meeting, Chris and I headed back to Kowloon and we had a chat in his office.

'Philip, this is my secretary, Mona. She does everything and is the boss around here. Be nice to her or you'll be in big trouble. Mona, this is Mr Nourse,' said Chris, pronouncing my name like *bourse*.

The Chinese can be very formal, addressing work colleagues by their family name, depending on their position in the hierarchy. Fortunately, the 'Mr Nourse' was dropped a day or two later.

'Mr Nourse, would you like a coffee – milk, sugar?'

'That would be lovely, Mona. Thank you. Milk but no sugar.'

Mona then delivered a cup of coffee topped up with condensed milk. This was the last time I drank white coffee for many years. Apparently, condensed milk was the norm.

I didn't really know what was expected of me. I was supposed to be setting up an Industrial Department, which I discovered meant an agency operation involving the sale and leasing of industrial property. David Runciman, another partner, who was the expert in industrial property, suggested I start by calling all the senior people in the top industrial companies to ascertain their property needs. The directory of industry was dumped on my desk. I made a number of calls and could not work out why I was not being taken seriously.

My first telephone call was to a Mr Wong Chi Leung, the finance director of Golden Star Industries Ltd.

'May I speak to Mr Leung, please?'

'Who you want speak to?' came the perplexed reply in Chinglish.

'Mr Leung,' I repeated.

'No Mr Leung here.' The line went dead.

I had no idea that the Chinese placed their family name first, so it was no wonder that I met with little success on my first few calls. I should have asked for Mr Wong. Traditionally, Chinese names are structured by a two-character pattern. The first part is the surname, shared by all members of a generation, and the last character is given to the individual. The Chinese write their surname first to show respect for their ancestors. I was beginning to learn how Hong Kong worked.

Robert, whom I visited in 1983, suggested I stay in his apartment in Mid-Levels until I found my own flat. I accepted his offer. As cargo manager of Cathay Pacific Airways, he travelled frequently and so I often had the place to myself. But when he was in Hong Kong, he looked after me well. We had a lot of fun – frequent barbecues on his balcony and regular visits to the FCC and other 'dubious' drinking establishments. He also had the use of his company's holiday houses and junk. We had many a fun trip to a colonial bungalow near Upper Cheung Sha Beach on Lantau Island, where a group of us would spend the weekend. On other occasions, Robert would invite us on the company junk and we would explore the outlying islands. He was very good to me.

In September 1984, I moved into 17C Monticello, 48 Kennedy Road in Mid-Levels. This was a lovely flat looking west across unbuilt areas with trees and greenery to Central District. I could see the tower of St John's Cathedral from my seventeenth-floor balcony. I spent a lot of time and money furnishing this flat and making it home. I bought a sofa, tables, bookshelves and beds from a rattan-furniture shop in Queen's Road East, run by an alluring Chinese girl called Possie, and explored Stanley Market and elsewhere, hunting for pictures. A beautiful home has always been important to me.

I made many friends. Early on, I was introduced to Stephanie Woolley, who lived in San Francisco Towers in Happy Valley, and she introduced me to Richard Gocher in a neighbouring flat. They were the first visitors, on 11th September 1984, to my newly furnished flat, followed soon afterwards by Robert, his then Japanese girlfriend, Keiko, and Chris Thrift. Through Lindsey Hamilton, who worked at Richard Ellis, I met Penny Fitzjohn and her partner, Brian, with whom I spent many happy times in the FCC. One of my colleagues in the office was Jenny Thomas, who looked after residential-property sales and lettings. She and her husband, Roger, were very kind to me. I am still in touch with all of these friends and Stephanie lives quite close to us in London, so we meet often.

I was having fun, but I was sometimes sad and homesick. I had made quite a few friends already but I would often sit up late at night, drinking whisky and playing Barbra Streisand's 'Heart Don't Change My Mind' over and over again, too loud. My poor downstairs neighbour wrote me a letter, asking me to turn down the volume. I was mortified, apologized in person and immediately bought some speaker stands.

I kept a diary, in which I recorded what I had been up to, extracts from which I used to send to my parents. I am not sure what they must have thought about my life in Hong Kong but, on rereading these extracts after my father died, I felt rather self-conscious and I destroyed them. (As I write this memoir, I realize how useful they would have been.)

*

My early impressions of Hong Kong will remain with me forever. It is one of the most exciting and dynamic cities in the world, with a geographical and cultural diversity that is unique – in clichéd terms, an exotic blend of East and West.

I first observed the trademark lifestyle of Hongkongers in the upper echelons of society: elegant and stylish fashion, a love of famous designer names, expensive motorcars (and yachts), an extravagant social life and conspicuous wealth.

Almost every expatriate and wealthy Chinese household had an amah (or domestic helper), more often than not from the Philippines, who worked long hours, six days a week. On Saturdays and Sundays, one would see thousands of amahs congregating in Central and other popular areas, picnicking, playing cards and engaging in myriad activities, sitting on cardboard boxes, to while away their precious day off. The noise of music and chitter-chatter amongst crowds of Filipinos can be deafening.

And yet Hong Kong had – and still has – a profound divide between rich and poor. The majority of ordinary people live on low incomes in tiny flats in high-rise buildings in some of the most densely populated areas anywhere in the world.

The contrast between Central District, the financial hub and home to upmarket office towers and shopping centres, and neighbouring Sheung Wan is extraordinary. One of the earliest British settlements, Sheung Wan is dominated by a maze of steep lanes and staircases, numerous food stalls and markets, traditional Chinese medicine shops, dried-seafood stalls, antique shops and art galleries. You no longer see the rickshaw pullers, sweating in the heat, but there are still hawkers and beggars. Man Mo Temple, one of the oldest temples in the city, is situated here; the incense coils burning ceaselessly, the fragrant smoke creating an almost spiritual atmosphere.

Hong Kong is a kaleidoscope. Dramatic skyscrapers, high-powered businesses and relentless entrepreneurial spirit rub shoulders with traditional villages, fishing communities and deep-rooted religious beliefs. And alongside this extraordinary cultural mix, Hong Kong offers an unspoilt landscape of staggering natural beauty, comparable in many ways with Scotland and parts of New Zealand.

Often regarded as no more than a concrete jungle, the urban areas of Hong Kong in fact account for less than twenty-five per cent of the territory and are concentrated on the north shore of Hong Kong Island, the Kowloon Peninsula and the New Territories. Astonishingly, forty per cent of the land area is designated as country parks and nature reserves.

I was fascinated by this cosmopolitan city of about 5.2 million people (1984): a medley of traditional Chinese culture, a world-famous harbour, spectacular countryside and state-of-the-art architecture. Unforgettable.

Ninety, eighty-four was a historic year for Hong Kong and the United Kingdom. The UK Government and the Government of the People's Republic of China signed the Sino-British Joint Declaration on the Question of Hong Kong, which would enable the transfer of sovereignty to China on 1st July 1997. In May 1985, the agreement was ratified and entered into force.

The background to this momentous event dates from the nineteenth century, when Hong Kong Island was ceded to Great Britain by China after the first Opium War in 1842. Further territory was added after the second Opium War and in 1898, when Great Britain obtained the New Territories on a ninety-nine-year lease.

I spent much of my working life with Richard Ellis travelling to the most far-flung industrial areas of Hong Kong in sweltering heat, dressed in a suit and tie, and waiting ten or fifteen minutes for a vast cargo lift in an ancient industrial building. The experience was extraordinary and I claim to know Hong Kong better than most of my peers – even to this day. I was reminded of my days inspecting the dark satanic mills in the north of England, but now I was more often than not in dilapidated high-rise buildings which probably would not have a hope of passing any kind of Health and Safety at Work regulations.

We worked hard but we also had fun. I had enormous respect for Chris Thrift, my boss in the Kowloon office. Shortly after I joined, we welcomed a young New Zealander, John, who was only about nineteen or twenty. We used to go to the White Stag for four pints of beer at lunchtime and get into all sorts of trouble after work. I was about fifteen years older than John but we spent a good deal of time together, meeting with friends for long lunches and very long evenings. Quite often, I did not get home until the early hours.

Social life in Hong Kong was – and indeed still is – a whirl: lunches and dinners with friends, parties, boat trips and the occasional flutter on the horses – a national pastime for Hongkongers – at one of Hong Kong's two racecourses.

For my first Christmas in Hong Kong, I was invited with some other friends to stay in a house in Kota Kinabalu in Sabah, a Malaysian state occupying the northern part of the island of Borneo. This was my first trip outside Hong Kong. We spent Christmas Day itself in a hotel training school upcountry, where one of our hosts worked. As you might expect, we enjoyed a veritable feast. We headed back to Kota Kinabalu for the New Year's Eve fancy-dress party at the Kinabalu Yacht Club. Unfortunately, I managed to lock the bathroom door from the outside while the girls were desperately trying to apply their warpaint before the party. I was in big trouble. Somehow, I managed to find a key after rummaging through numerous drawers and all was saved – including me.

Over the Easter holiday in 1985, I went to Puerto Galera in the Philippines with Penny and Brian and another friend, Marilyn. Puerto Galera is south of Manila on the island of Mindoro.

After a very uncomfortable three-hour drive to Batangas, we took a banker, a small timber boat with outriggers, to reach our destination. It was here that I met Vida, an attractive Filipina girl who was holidaying with the owners (whom I knew) of a curiously named bar called Bottoms Up in Tsimshatsui. We became romantically involved and I went to see her in Manila. It later transpired that she had a boyfriend who 'had a gun'. Anxious, she advised me that he was planning to visit Hong Kong over Chinese New Year in 1986. I honestly don't think he had any intention of looking me up – I doubt he even knew anything about me. Nonetheless, I decided to visit Guangzhou in southern China over the New Year holiday. I didn't see her again but she told me she was marrying her boyfriend and going to live in America.

I was not suited to agency work – doing deals – and I have always known that. I may be a good salesman but I am not a deal closer. It is not in my blood. Of course, I had been working in fee-earning environments with both Jones Lang Wootton and Weatherall Green & Smith, but there I was undertaking professional work whereas at Richard Ellis I was involved in sales and leasing. I was under some pressure from the partners to earn fees.

One afternoon in the Richard Ellis box at the Hong Kong Sevens,* Michael Hollington, one of the partners, said to me, 'Look, Nourse, you're not making enough bloody money. You need to bring in half a million by the end of the year.' Michael, who is a good friend and lives nearby in Barnes with his wife, Sarah, still addresses me as Nourse to this day.

---

* *The world-famous annual rugby event, which celebrated its tenth Hong Kong anniversary in 1985.*

With Christopher (right) in Moffat, 1962

Sailing *Falcon*, Seaton, circa 1964

My mother visiting Marlborough
College, 1964

Me (left), my mother, my father and
Christopher outside No 10
The Cloisters, Garter Day, 1965

No 24 The Cloisters, our second home in Windsor Castle
(with the Singer Gazelle), 1967

Our small house (to the right with the bay windows) in the precincts of Canterbury Cathedral. My father's office was immediately above the Christ Church Gate on the left, 1969

From left: Christopher, Jennie, Tooki, my cousin Frank, me and Sylvie, Seaton, 1969

My first and last beard, Spetses, Greece, 1978

Sarah, Kew Gardens, October 1983

With my mother in the Foreign Correspondents' Club, Hong Kong, October 1989

With Di at Giraffe Manor, Kenya, January 1990

Chesterton Petty staff annual dinner, Hong Kong, 1991

With Hanifa, my marketing assistant, in Jardine House, Hong Kong, 1991

With Richard, setting sail for
Shanghai, June 1991

Me (left), my father, my mother and
Christopher in Devon on my father's
69th birthday, 28th August 1991

Our marriage, St Stephen's Chapel, Hong Kong, 8th November 1991

The family gathering after my mother's funeral, Lympstone, 29th May 1992

Our first junk, Lamma Island, December 1992

Leather wedding anniversary, Royal Hong Kong Yacht Club, November 1994

With my father, Lympstone, October 1996

Me (left) with Di, Robert and Julie at the Queen's Birthday Cocktails, Hong Kong Club, 13th June 1998

On top of the Franz Josef Glacier, New Zealand, February 1999

Sarah and my father at my 50th birthday party in the Oriental Club, London,
October 1999

My 50th birthday party, Hong Kong Club, October 1999

From left: Michael, me, David,
Angus and Gerry on board our junk,
April 2001

My exhibition for the China
Coast Community Charity Ball at
Government House, Hong Kong,
March 2003

From left: Charles, Sarah, me, Di, Father and Christopher at Christopher's flat in
Queen's Gate, London, September 2004

I did not reply to Michael's exhortation. I was not happy at Richard Ellis because I knew that I could not cut the mustard. I had been looking around for a new opportunity anyway. I was disillusioned by the property business – as I was way back in the early days of JLW. I wanted something completely different.

I was quietly in discussion with Peat Marwick Management Consultants, who were looking for a senior person to run their Executive Recruitment Division. I had no experience but the prospect of working in a completely new field attracted me. I think the partners of Peat Marwick also found the prospect of an 'outsider' rather refreshing. I was offered and accepted the position of manager in Peat Marwick in June 1985.

After leaving Richard Ellis, I headed back to England for a holiday. I decided to spend a week in Sri Lanka en route and flew Air Lanka (now SriLankan Airlines) to Colombo, the commercial capital of the former British colony, which gained independence in 1948. I stayed for two nights in the Galle Face Hotel, built by the British in 1864 and once listed as one of the '1000 Places to See Before You Die' in the book of the same name. Colombo was a port on the ancient East-West trade routes and its heritage is reflected in its colonial architecture.

Since driving oneself in Sri Lanka was out of the question – the roads were appalling and the driving far too dangerous – I picked up a car with a driver and we set off for Kandy and Nuwara Eliya, set in the hill country and home to numerous tea plantations. I stayed in the famous Hill Club where I was overawed: a real log fire burning in the bedroom and white-gloved waiters tiptoeing around the grand dining room providing first-class silver service. The hotels all had quarters for drivers who seemed to be well looked after.

The following day, we set off for another long drive to Yala on the south coast, famous for its National Park. Yala was one of the areas worst hit by the Boxing Day 2004 tsunami, in which 35,000 people sadly lost their lives in Sri Lanka alone. (I was in Phuket, Thailand, during the tsunami, which was also badly affected.) I spent two or three nights here, visiting the National Park and simply relaxing and walking along the beautiful beach. Time to reflect: I was now well established in Hong Kong and was looking forward to seeing family and friends in England before returning to a new career.

Our last stop was Galle, another colonial town inscribed as a World Heritage site in 1988, where I stayed at another beautiful hotel, the name of which I am unable to recall and cannot find in my research – very probably due to a name change.

At the end of the trip, my driver insisted I meet his family. I was a little hesitant but knew this was quite usual when foreigners hired drivers. He took me to his very modest home where I met his wife and two young children. They offered me tea and biscuits and were so kind and sincere. It was truly a privilege to have been invited into their home and to see how they lived.

During my stay in England, I spent time with Sarah, who was now nearly five. We stayed with my parents in their house in Hythe (bought for later retirement) and Sarah stayed with me in Richmond. I used to write to her from Hong Kong but, not having seen me for a year, she was not surprisingly shy at the beginning and probably felt a little insecure. However, she relaxed quickly enough and we enjoyed ourselves on the beach in Hythe and in Kew Gardens, just across the road from my flat and one of our favourite spots.

After a week or two in England, I returned to Hong Kong and joined Peat Marwick Management Consultants in July. The set-up and atmosphere were very different from what I was used to. The people and the culture were completely alien to me after having been in the property industry (with which I was disillusioned) for so long. We had to fill in time sheets and you could not even obtain a new pencil or pad of paper without explaining yourself to Alice, the all-important admin lady who had probably been employed since before most of us were born.

Stan Miller, my boss, was quite a character and we got on well. He introduced me to many clients, mainly in the financial sector, and I was able to secure and complete a number of high-level recruitment assignments. Unlike negotiating a property transaction, the process did not involve the 'sell' – rather, establishing a good rapport with my clients, gaining their respect and giving constructive professional advice.

I had a staff of three or four, including my secretary, Stella, who was very forward and outspoken, and Ambrose Chan, who we all assumed was very wealthy. He was small in stature, but he spoke impeccable English, dressed in expensive suits and radiated charm and sophistication. He subsequently married an American and went to live in the States. We all worked well together. I also had two English colleagues who worked on the same floor: James, who looked after the Financial Services Division, and Roger, who ran the IT Consultancy. I have no idea what happened to James but I still keep in touch with Roger, who lives in Islington.

I quickly discovered, to my surprise, that 'accountants' in general were simply not my type. Their culture was quite different from what I was used to; they did not seem to have the presence of my property colleagues. That said, I made some good friends and we used to enjoy regular trips to Macau and long Friday lunches with steak tartare, followed by too much port, in the original Chinnery Bar at the Mandarin Oriental hotel.

I was sent to an international Peat Marwick conference in Chicago in 1986. On the first evening, I met a girl who claimed to be the daughter of the owner of the hotel. She took me off to some of Chicago's wonderful blues bars before returning for a late-night hamburger. The following morning, I was a little late for the conference proceedings but still managed to give my PowerPoint presentation on executive recruitment in the Far East.

During 1986, I visited Bangkok at least once. This fun, fast-paced city is well known for its culinary delights, including outstanding Thai food, shopping and, of course, its red-light districts which are swarming with young working girls (and ladyboys).

I also made the annual pilgrimage to England to see Sarah, family and friends. Elaine was kind enough to host a party for me at her home in Teddington. It was a special occasion, full of laughter and warmth, a reunion with the Teddington crowd and other friends too.

In the autumn of 1986, I moved into a new flat, also in Monticello, and I bought a Roland electric piano with a rhythm box. This gave me many hours of pleasure and the opportunity to practise playing once again.

By this time, Di had come back into my life. She followed me to Hong Kong in the autumn of 1984, a few months after I had landed. She did not get in touch with me until later; the story goes that I apparently knew she was in Hong Kong because a friend of mine, who was in the recruitment business, showed me her CV. She then obtained a job with Baker & McKenzie, a multinational law firm, as a temporary secretary.

Di did eventually contact me sometime in 1986 and we met for a drink on a few occasions in Culture Club, a modern chic bar with a Japanese restaurant, on the top floor of Pedder Building in Central. And then on one such occasion in late 1986, Di asked me if she could stay in my spare room as the flat she was sharing with others was being sold. I said yes and she moved in sometime after Christmas.

A day or two before Christmas, I held a cocktail party for about twenty-five people in my flat. I brought in all the drinks but asked the FCC to provide canapés and waiters. It was a good party and, of course, continued late into the evening. Apparently, I did not invite Di and she was rather hurt.

Although still rocky, we began to rebuild our relationship. The turning point was when I asked her if she would like to come with me to Penang over the Easter holiday. Di was happy and we spent a very enjoyable few days relaxing in the sun.

Peat Marwick was a huge risk for both the partners of the firm and me. I found it difficult to fit into the 'accountancy' culture and I became somewhat weary of interviewing candidates, the majority of whom were accountants. It turned out to be a mistake and we parted company amicably in July 1987.

After I left Peat Marwick, I was involved in two editorial projects – one a book about tantric Buddhism! – but my main focus was on finding a new job. I spoke to a number of property firms, including Chesterton Petty, but the prospects did not look good. I knew I was disillusioned with the property world, but it was what I knew, and the people were so much more interesting than the average accountant.

On 19th October, stock markets crashed, with the Dow Jones Industrial Average falling 22.6 per cent, the largest one-day percentage drop in its history. The Hang Seng Index in Hong Kong declined by more than forty per cent that October. This memorable day became known as Black Monday.

In this climate, there was absolutely no prospect of employment and I decided to pack my bags and call it a day. I was very sad that my time in Hong Kong was coming to an end after just a little over three years. Di helped me pack up the flat and, once again, we said goodbye. She was still living with me and planned to go and stay with friends in Pokfulam. I should note that her help was invaluable since I had not long before slipped in the shower and managed to break two or three ribs.

I flew back to England – on the same flight as Robert, as it happened, which had the advantage of an upgrade to First Class. My father picked me up at Gatwick Airport very early in the morning and we drove back to Charing, where my parents were now settled in their new vicarage (completed in 1986). I remember my father pointing out some of the devastation caused by the 'Great Storm of 1987', which occurred a few days before Black Monday – a prescient warning of what was to come, perhaps.

Chapter 7
Interregnum

1987-1988

I was a little depressed. To all intents, I had failed in Hong Kong. I was reminded of the Hong Kong acronym: FILTH – Failed In London, Try Hong Kong! My dream of living and working abroad had not really worked. My parents, of course, were concerned that Hong Kong did not seem to have worked out but were delighted to have me home in Charing. I enjoyed some rest time, but I could not sleep and ended up taking some sort of sleeping pills for several months.

Assuming that there was no future in Hong Kong, I started looking for a job in the autumn of 1987. After the Peat Marwick experience, the property industry was the top of my list, but it proved difficult because I had been absent for more than three years and I was effectively 'out of the market'. I was up and down to London on a regular basis and I went to see Kenneth Easter, my old boss at Jones Lang Wootton, to ask if there might be a position for me back in JLW.

He looked at me quizzically and said, 'I think the best thing you can do, Philip, is to go back to Hong Kong.' Harsh words, perhaps, but he was right, as he so often was.

Ironically, perhaps, I was welcomed into the executive-recruitment field because I had experience, maturity and the right personality. The Royal Institution of Chartered Surveyors, of which I was of course a member, ran a recruitment division for property people, and the director in charge was very keen for me to take over his position since he was due to retire. Another opportunity arose through a friend, Peter Venn, who owned a recruitment agency called Surveyors Consultancy Services. He suggested I might buy the business. For various reasons, neither of these leads worked out.

However, I was offered jobs at a medium-sized firm of accountants, which specialized in recruitment, and Touche Ross Management Consultants, one of the 'Big Eight' in those days. The firm is known today as Deloitte Touche Tohmatsu, one of the 'Big Four' (owing to never-ending mergers). I was somewhat hesitant about joining an accountancy firm again but Touche Ross Management Consultants was a vast independent business in its own right and seemed quite remote from the accountancy arm.

I was like Buridan's ass starving between two stacks of hay. On the one hand, the smaller firm was offering me a higher salary (and a better car); on the other hand, I had the opportunity to join a well-established international firm which would offer greater security and perhaps more camaraderie in the workplace. So keen was the smaller firm to take me on that they insisted I have a trial week in the office to see how I felt. In the end, it was an easy decision: the office seemed dark and lonely and I knew that I would not hack it. So I accepted the offer from Touche Ross and started work in Holborn Circus at the beginning of 1988.

The tenants in my flat in Richmond were not due to leave until March, so Susan, who was such a good friend to Elaine and me in Teddington, offered me the spare room in her house in Alder Road,

Mortlake. I accepted this kind offer and I started commuting to Waterloo, taking the bus to Fetter Lane and walking up to the office.

It took me a little time to settle in to the heavy routine of interviewing candidates for a variety of jobs – sometimes in the finance sector but also in other fields – but the work gave me satisfaction and I got on well with my colleagues. There were only about eight people in the office but we enjoyed the camaraderie that is so important. I became very good friends with two of the girls, Celia and Frances, and keep in touch with Frances, who emigrated to New Zealand, to this day.

In the spring, I settled back into my flat in Richmond and redecorated it – top to bottom. I also received a delivery of some of the furniture I had shipped back from Hong Kong. The flat was shipshape and looking rather good: some new furniture, curtains from Peter Jones and so on. I also bought a folding bicycle, which enabled me to wobble back from dinner parties a little the worse for wear without the risk of losing my driving licence – a worthwhile investment!

Although I kept in touch with Di, speaking on the telephone from time to time, I was surprised one day when she contacted me and said she was coming to London for Easter. I was not at all unhappy and met her at the airport. On the way home, we bought hot cross buns in the bakery at the bottom of Kew Road. We had a fun time and then she returned to her job with Price Waterhouse in Hong Kong. She subsequently asked her boss, Henry Lum, for a sabbatical of several months and came back to Richmond in the late summer.

At the time, I was seeing Liz, whom I knew because she was a good friend of Susan. We became quite close at Susan's birthday party in early July and started spending time together. We even went to Spain with Susan and her boyfriend, Colin, now her husband. I had given myself a serious dilemma. I had to make a decision. I sadly broke up with Liz. We were both genuinely very upset but I knew I had made the right decision.

Di and I bumped into Liz at Colin's sixtieth birthday party in 2016, twenty-eight years on, and she seemed a little distant. She told me shortly afterwards that it felt like unfinished business. According to Di, it was only after that party that she found out about my relationship with Liz.

Di stayed with me for several months. After so many ups and downs and breaks in our relationship, we were very much one and we decided that we would stay together for good. I am not sure how Di was planning to square this with Henry Lum but, as it happens, there was no need.

We spent time with my family, visiting my parents in Charing and then Hythe, on the Kent coast, where my father retired in September 1988, and seeing Sarah at weekends. We also caught up with my brother, Christopher, and Di's mother, with whom she had never been close, and her siblings, John and Shirley. We had always kept in close touch with friends so there was a great deal of socializing.

One day in early September, I received a call from Gordon Moffoot, a director of Chesterton Petty in Hong Kong, with whom I had spoken in 1987.

'Is that Philip?'

'Yes, it is.'

'This is Gordon Moffoot, Chesterton Petty in Hong Kong. You remember you came to see me and Paul Varty last year?'

'Yes, of course I remember, Gordon.'

'Well, we were talking about you earlier this morning and Paul asked me to give you a call. We want to set up a new Research and Marketing Division and wonder if you would be interested.'

After a brief pause, I replied, 'Most certainly, I would. What exactly have you got in mind?'

'Well, we need to increase our profile in the market and want to publish research reports on the various property sectors – you know, residential, offices, retail and so on.'

'Yes, I understand.'

'And also, someone who can improve our marketing generally.'

'I would definitely be interested but obviously we'd need to talk further. Where do we go from here?'

'Could you come out to Hong Kong and we can discuss it in more detail and hopefully work out some terms?'

'Yes, I can do that. Can I look at some dates and get back to you?'

'Yes, of course. Give me a call as soon as you can.'

The long and the short of it was that I flew to Hong Kong later that month to discuss the position and was offered the job.

I don't think we had a chance to meet during my short visit but I always remember speaking on the phone to Chris Thrift, my former Richard Ellis boss, while I was there and mentioning that it was my daughter Sarah's eighth birthday. Chris said to me repeatedly, 'Call your daughter, call your daughter.' I didn't. I couldn't because I really didn't want Elaine or Sarah to know I was back in Hong Kong. I am not sure how either would have reacted to my apparent desire to return to Hong Kong after settling back in England and seeing Sarah on a regular basis.

Di and I were going back to Hong Kong. We were both thrilled and happy to be making a commitment to each other – finally. My parents were not happy about our departure, understandably, but we knew we had to go. Executive recruitment was not really for me, and I was excited by the prospect of returning to the city I loved and moving back into the property industry after three and a half years in the wilderness.

We left Richmond shortly before Christmas in 1988. Stewart Reading-Kitchen, a good friend, insisted on driving us to the airport, even though his tiny car could scarcely accommodate the vast quantities of luggage we had. As we left, Mrs Elsey, my wonderful ground-floor neighbour, waved from her window. She looked very sad, as indeed was I. We sent her a postcard from Hong Kong a month or two later but she never received it. Her daughter, Dolina, told us she had died.

Leaving England once again, I felt enormous guilt about Sarah, who was now eight years old. I had seen her regularly, of course, but Elaine was by now married to Peter Smith and life seemed good. Nonetheless, I was concerned that I had not been a real father to my daughter and this sense of guilt haunted me always.

Sarah was now known by the name of Smith, which I was not happy about, and in July 1990 I received a letter from Elaine's solicitors proposing that Sarah should be adopted by her and Peter. This I resisted vehemently because I felt it was quite wrong and unnecessary. I replied to her solicitors asking for an explanation of the past history on which they based their advice that adoption would be the correct course. The application for an adoption order was later dropped. There followed a proposal for sole custody, to which I gave my consent, but this was not pursued. The granting of sole custody to Elaine would not have affected my visitation rights. In the event, Elaine and Peter subsequently separated. My decision not to consent to adoption was undoubtedly right.

Chapter 8
Back to Hong Kong

1988-1993

In December 1988, Di and I arrived back in Hong Kong – a fresh start. I had a new job with Chesterton Petty, back in the property world, and Di was able to take up her previous position in the Tax Department of Price Waterhouse. Chesterton Petty had recently moved into a new office covering the entire twenty-eighth floor of Jardine House in Central. Opened in 1973, it was Hong Kong's first skyscraper and the tallest building in Asia at the time. The fifty-two-storey building is adorned with 1,750 circular windows and is known in the vernacular as 'the building of a thousand arseholes'.

My dear friend, Robert, asked us to stay with him (I also stayed with him in 1984) in his apartment in Wang Fung Terrace in Tai Hang, close to the Causeway Bay area. We probably overstayed our welcome – two or three months – but we had enormous fun. He had a very attractive girlfriend, Cora, who was an air hostess with Cathay Pacific in First Class.

He had a large older-style apartment – elegant with high ceilings but unmodernized – with a terrace where we used to sit with drinks and often have barbecues. On one occasion, Cora was sitting on Robert's knee and the whole chair crumpled under them. There were no injuries and we all roared with laughter. It should be said that Robert was rather overweight, and the lightweight garden chair was not built for the combined weight of Robert and Cora, although she was very slim.

We spent Christmas with Robert in Wang Fung Terrace. He had to travel on business shortly afterwards. Di and I decided to invite friends, including Robert Grinter, Barbara Waters and Viswa Nathan, round for dinner on New Year's Eve, following which we headed down to the Foreign Correspondents' Club to see in the New Year. At some point late in the evening, Robert returned from his travels and joined us in the FCC.

Robert Grinter worked for the Independent Commission Against Corruption, a government body set up in 1974 to fight rampant corruption in the public sector. The story goes that ambulance crews would demand 'tea money' before picking up a sick person; and the chief police superintendent slipped out of the territory while under investigation for acquiring unearned wealth of over HK$4 million from corrupt means. Robert was always very secretive about his work – a requirement of his senior position.

He lived in government quarters that were rather special – a lovely colonial-style bungalow with a large garden on Mount Butler Road. He invited us for a barbecue shortly after Christmas – perhaps on New Year's Day – insisting he cook on his rather primitive brazier, rather than a modern barbecue. It was a long, fun day.

Later in January, friends from England, Stewart and Judy Reading-Kitchen, were passing through Hong Kong and Robert, with whom we were still staying, invited us all to one of the Swire holiday houses in Shek Kong in the New Territories. We had a splendid weekend, swimming and walking, but I think we were all pretty inebriated on the Saturday night. There are photographs of us all climbing up the garden wall in various states of undress after a barbecue supper. I have no idea what the amahs must have thought the following morning; probably best forgotten.

I had been appointed as a manager at Chesterton Petty with responsibility for setting up the new Research and Marketing Division. I had a marketing assistant, Hanifa Mak, who worked with me for several years, and various research staff who prepared reports on the local property market and specific subjects of topical interest. One of our first publications, produced in conjunction with a lecturer at the University of Hong Kong, was entitled *A Yen for a Yen*, an in-depth report on the flight of capital out of Japan at this time. I was also responsible for corporate promotion, company publications and brochures, advertising and public relations.

I had a very good relationship with the chairman and directors of the company, although one of the directors (who must remain anonymous) was somewhat sceptical about my suitability for the job. His view was that the position called for a 'professional researcher', someone with an economics or property-research background, which I did not have. He had a point and was not always supportive of me, sometimes sidestepping me. Fortunately, he was outvoted by the other directors, who promoted me to senior associate in 1989 and executive director a year later. The irony of the situation was that I survived longer than he did. He left the board a year or two before I left the company in 2005.

Di and I were looking for a suitable apartment while we were staying with Robert. We looked at countless properties in our preferred locations and in March 1989 took on a lovely apartment in Greenery Garden, a brand-new development in Mount Davis Road, Pokfulam, a quiet, leafy area fifteen minutes' drive west of Central District. We were one of the early occupants of the block. The flat had a large living area with a semi-circular balcony, big enough to entertain six people to supper. The view was stunning – looking west across the West Lamma Channel towards Lantau Island. The kitchen was a little on the small side but we managed perfectly well. In addition, there were three bedrooms and two bathrooms. In front of the block was a swimming pool, which I used regularly.

Di and I used to take the 3A bus from outside our block into Central for the first few months but, after I was promoted, I had the benefit of a company car, so we would drive to work and usually try and meet up for the return journey.

Several of our friends had already moved into Greenery Garden, including Nigel de Boinville, who was a bachelor and a struggling barrister. Nigel had a reputation for never buying a drink and was often seen roaming the Foreign Correspondents' Club, hoping that a generous member would offer him libation. He lived a few floors above us in the adjoining block. On Sundays, when we usually enjoyed a traditional roast, he would detect the whiff of roasting meat drifting upwards and lean over from his balcony.

'Can I pop down for a drink?' he would suggest.

'Yes, of course, come and have a quick pre-prandial sherry,' we would answer.

He invariably stayed for the duration.

On 4th June 1989, following weeks of democracy protests and demonstrations in Beijing and elsewhere in China by university students calling for political reform, tanks rumbled through the capital's streets and Chinese troops stormed Tiananmen Square in the centre of the city, killing or wounding thousands of protesters and arresting thousands more. The brutal government assault, which became known as the Tiananmen Square Massacre, shocked the West and brought denunciations from the United States, the Soviet Union and elsewhere. A few weeks later, the United States imposed economic sanctions on the People's Republic of China. The people of Hong Kong were shell-shocked by the events and vigils are held on 4th June every year (with the exception of 2020 due to social-distancing restrictions imposed because of the coronavirus).

At the time the news broke in Hong Kong, I was having a drink with colleagues in the boardroom of our Jardine House office. Di was in her office in Prince's Building on the other side of Connaught Road Central. Prince's Building was about to be locked down and Di, one of the last people in the office, was desperately trying to get hold of me. Finally, we made contact and met in the car park to drive home. Such was our concern over the events that had just taken place, we decided to drive home through the Mid-Levels area, popular with expatriates, rather than via Sai Ying Pun and Kennedy Town, which were much more 'local' areas.

Interestingly, five months later, during a wave of democratization that swept through Eastern Europe and ultimately resulted in the demolition of the Berlin Wall – portrayed by the Eastern Bloc as protecting its population from fascist elements conspiring to prevent the 'will of the people' – the East German government opened the country's borders with West Germany and West Berlin.

Since we had not made any holiday arrangements in 1989, we made a last-minute decision to go to Sarawak, a Malaysian state adjoining Sabah (where I spent Christmas in 1984) on the island of Borneo, for a week in September. We stayed in a beautiful beachfront hotel a short distance outside Kuching, the rather drab capital.

We spent most of our time relaxing in the hotel, enjoying leisurely meals and sunbathing. In those days, we both smoked and would sit at our outside breakfast table for at least an hour, reading or putting the world to rights and smoking far too many cigarettes. Before sunset, we used to go on to the beach at low tide, where I took numerous photographs of the sun setting before drinks and an al fresco dinner, accompanied by the ceaseless chirping of crickets.

It was here that Di saw me in my true colours. We were shown to a room in a medium-rise block in our hotel. But when I looked at the view from the room, I could see many attractive stand-alone villas set amongst the lush gardens. I asked to be moved but, after a short time, I felt the new room was dark and depressing so we moved to another villa right on the beachfront. I forget what the problem was with our third room but, to cut a long story short, we ended up back in the room where we started. So we moved room three times during quite a short holiday.

Of course, Di knows me rather better now and usually expects to move room or change table in a restaurant at least once. I should add that I now take a note of room numbers in hotels where we have stayed for future reference; in the case of restaurants, I either know my preferred table number or select a table when booking in person.

During the summer, my mother announced that she was going to visit Di and me in Hong Kong. I think she had toyed with the idea since we left a year earlier, knowing that my father would not make the long journey. Father, Christopher, Di and I were gobsmacked. My mother, aged sixty-seven, was surely not capable of making such a trip on her own and certainly lacked the confidence and savvy to do so. I recall Christopher saying it would never happen. Despite all our misgivings, my mother did make the trip in October (fortunately, with an upgrade to Business Class, courtesy of Robert) and I duly picked her up at Kai Tak Airport and brought her home to Greenery Garden.

She loved it; she seemed as happy as a sandboy. Di and I were both working, although I took some time off, but she needed no entertainment. She was happy to sit on the balcony, looking at the ships passing by, and would often meet us in the Foreign Correspondents' Club after work, having come in by bus – a remarkable feat in itself. I would walk into the main bar and there was my mother, with an air of confidence I had never seen before, propping up the bar with a large glass of alcohol-free wine (as she was not drinking). I think that Mother had more pluck than we gave her credit for and perhaps my father was too ready to criticize. She probably felt rather put down.

I celebrated my fortieth birthday on 21st October 1989. We were having a black-tie dinner in the wood-panelled Ward Room of the Royal Hong Kong Yacht Club, of which I was (and still am) a member. My mother asked me if I would mind very much if she did not join the dinner. Despite the apparent self-confidence, I think she was nervous about meeting all sorts of strangers. I tried to persuade her to come but she clearly did not want to and I did not press the matter. She waited up until we were home. She enjoyed the post-mortem and we opened my presents over a celebratory drink.

Di and I had bought a share in a junk earlier in the year. I had studied for my Master's and Engineer's Certificate at the Royal Hong Kong Yacht Club in 1986 and was awarded a Pleasure Vessel Certificate of Competency. This allowed me to skipper the boat solo, although Ah Lai, our boat boy, was generally at the helm since I was not entirely confident in manoeuvring a forty-two-foot boat in tricky waters.

We took my mother out on several occasions. The junk was large and, although Mother was never a lover of the sea or boats, she felt entirely comfortable. She thoroughly enjoyed it. I have video recordings of these outings but, sadly, I can no longer play them.

We also showed her some of the nightlife of Hong Kong. She was game for anything, it seemed, and happily chatted to every Tom, Dick and Harry.

My mother had not travelled abroad very much – our trips to Sweden, Italy and Austria and two to France without me – so coming to Hong Kong on her own was an extraordinary achievement, a trip that she remembered with enormous pleasure and pride for the few remaining years of her life.

*

Chesterton Petty's Property Management Division was based in our Kowloon office in Tsimshatsui. We managed about seventy properties, the majority residential but with several high-class commercial buildings. Paul Varty, my managing director, was not happy with the performance of the individual running the division and asked me to review the operation and involve myself as necessary. This was not a derogation of my existing responsibilities. However, as I was running the Research and Marketing Division, which was not a fee-earning operation, it was felt that I would be the most suitable person to undertake the task.

I spent two or three afternoons a week in the Kowloon office and quickly realized that the individual in charge was not the right person and that there was little focus on business development. He was a little paranoid. Justiner Wong, who was his secretary and continued to work in the Property Management Division until 2020, once told me that he had a large tape recorder under his desk and recorded every telephone conversation. We might expect this in today's world but not in the early 1990s.

The division was profitable but there was little prospect of expanding the business or increasing profits. We were just ticking over. Paul and I decided that he should go, so he was called into Paul's office after work one day and Paul asked him to resign. He seemed very relaxed – almost relieved, I think.

The downside of this decision was that responsibility for the division now ultimately rested with me. I cannot say that I relished the thought of being further involved in property management – hardly the most stimulating aspect of the property industry, albeit one of the most important. I now had two divisions under my wing. However, with the support of senior staff running the day-to-day operations, it was perfectly manageable.

Not long after, we decided to close the office in Kowloon and move the property-management team into Jardine House, which made life a great deal more convenient for me as I could easily alternate between my two roles. The staff were generally happy to be back in the head office.

My friends, Penny and Brian, whom I met when I first arrived in Hong Kong in 1984 and who left the territory in 1987, had returned to Kenya where they were brought up. They were now running Giraffe Manor on the outskirts of Nairobi near Nairobi National Park. How they came to be running a luxury lodge I am not sure, but I recall that the owner was perhaps a friend and had asked them to take it over for a year or two. Penny and Brian had suggested that we should come to Kenya at Chinese New Year 1989, which was in early February. However, because I had only joined Chesterton Petty at the end of 1988, I felt that it would be too soon to take a lengthy holiday. We therefore agreed we would go early in 1990.

So, shortly after New Year, Di and I set off for our eagerly anticipated trip to Kenya. We decided to spend a night in Bombay (officially Mumbai since 1995), staying at the luxury Taj Mahal Palace hotel. In November 2008, the Taj Mahal, probably Mumbai's best hotel, was the target of a terrorist attack. Hostages were taken and many people were killed, including foreigners.

Unfortunately, when we arrived at Sahar International Airport, there was no sign of Di's luggage. It transpired that it had been mistakenly sent to London. We had just come from a rather cool Hong Kong to a humid thirty degrees in Bombay so she had no suitable clothes and we had to spend most of the day shopping, with great difficulty, for all her essentials.

We left the hotel the following day, still with no sign of the errant luggage. I was suffering from food poisoning acquired from eating a curry the night before at the Taj Mahal. We were shocked on our way to the airport early in the morning to see such appalling conditions and poverty on the roadside – even people defecating.

Happily, Di's suitcase reappeared before we left Bombay. She saw the luggage arriving from London while we waited for our delayed flight to Nairobi and managed to retrieve it – just in time.

Penny and Brian picked us up at the airport and took us to Giraffe Manor. What a magical place – built in 1932 in the style of a Scottish hunting lodge and set in extensive grounds where the owners ran a breeding programme to reintroduce an endangered population of Rothschild giraffe into the wild.

The giraffes were very tame and happily poked their heads through the front door and even the first-floor windows of the manor. We used to sit at breakfast and feed them as they stretched their necks through the windows into the dining room.

During our stay, we attended what was probably the first public burning of rhinoceros horns. This symbolic protest against the killing of endangered species and trade in ivory and rhino horns was organized by well-known anthropologist and conservationist Richard Leakey in Nairobi National Park. Kenya's president, Daniel arap Moi, set the huge pile of horns alight with a burning torch. As a result, Kenya was able to convince a majority of the world's countries to ban the international trade in ivory and rhino horns, largely fuelled by Chinese demand for jewellery, carvings and traditional medicines that claim to offer healing properties.

I reported on this remarkable event, and my article and photographs were published in the May 1990 issue of *The Correspondent*, the Foreign Correspondents' Club's monthly magazine.

One evening, Penny and Brian took us for dinner at the Muthaiga Country Club, once described as 'the Moulin Rouge of Africa' during colonial times, where the elite 'drank champagne and pink gin for breakfast, played cards, danced through the night, and generally woke up with someone else's spouse in the morning'.

Here we were in the centre of Africa and yet the absence of any black people in the dining room, other than waiting staff, was conspicuous. We were shocked. Although Kenya was opposed to South Africa's policy of apartheid, which was still in force in 1990, a policy of institutionalized racial segregation, emanating from colonial days, was still practised in Kenya. (The legislation governing apartheid in South Africa was repealed in 1991.)

After several days, the four of us took a small plane to the Maasai Mara National Reserve, one of the finest and most diverse wildlife reserves in Africa, which adjoins the Serengeti National Park in Tanzania. We stayed in Little Governors' Camp, a luxury tented retreat situated around a watering hole that was teeming with wildlife. The camp was only accessible by a short boat ride across the crocodile-infested Mara River. Apparently, the location of the camp was considered so good that in colonial times it was reserved for the colonial governors of Kenya; hence its name.

We were taken out on safari early each morning and also in the late afternoon. The opportunities for photography were, of course, exceptional. We regularly spotted the Big Five: lion, elephant, rhino, leopard and buffalo; as well as cheetah, giraffe, hippo and zebra. One night, we were disturbed by unusual sounds and felt an animal brushing against the sides of our tent. On further investigation, it turned out to be a hippo casually wandering down to the watering hole – a potentially very dangerous situation. Apparently, the hippo regularly wandered into the camp to raid the bins.

We were served three grand meals a day by white-gloved waiters, with silver service, on the finest table linen. Sherry was served before dinner.

The experience of Maasai Mara was unforgettable – even thirty years later. I would love to return one day; if not to The Mara, to another of Africa's spectacular game reserves.

After ten magical days, we said our goodbyes to Penny and

Brian and set off on the final leg of our Kenyan journey: to Malindi on the east coast, where we stayed in a rather primitive beach house owned by a Hong Kong barrister. We were literally yards from the beach, which at night was teeming with tiny crabs burrowing their way through the white sand. There were two servants who belonged to the household and did all the shopping, cooking, cleaning and any other chores.

On our first full day, we foolishly collected a rental car from an unknown company. We were stopped by a very large, African policeman on the way back to the beach. He peered through the passenger window, having seen that the car did not have a tax disc.

'This vehicle is not taxed,' he said. 'I charge you.'

Somewhat taken aback, Di replied, 'How much?' She assumed that he meant to give us an on-the-spot fine.

'Are you trying to bribe me?' he retorted, while writing out some sort of charge sheet and adding that we would have to go to court.

I was somewhat alarmed at the prospect of having to attend court and languishing in an African jail. Having decided to write a letter of explanation to the local judge, I then tried to deliver it by hand to the court where he was presiding. This was a challenge. After fighting my way through throngs of what I presumed were hardened criminals awaiting trial, I marched right into the courtroom and courteously laid my letter on the judge's bench. He looked at it – and possibly read it – and he then dismissed me from the court. I remained concerned that we would perhaps be stopped at the airport when we left the country. However, that was the last I heard of the matter and we breathed a sigh of relief once our plane had taken off.

At some point during our time in Malindi, our very good Hong Kong friend, Richard Gocher, joined us. He was on his way to Johannesburg in South Africa where he worked in the 1970s. We enjoyed several days together, walking along the beach, eating, drinking and playing Monopoly.

While we were in Malindi, we observed many metal signs, attached to buildings and elsewhere, with vivid illustrations clearly reflecting the government's war on alcohol abuse and the 'evils of drink'. Richard tells me that some shops were selling these signs; apparently, we bought one or two to bring home, although neither of us can find any evidence of them now.

Flying back to Hong Kong via Bombay, we had another bad experience. Having spent most of the night waiting for our flight to Hong Kong, the airport staff went on strike shortly before we were due to pick up our boarding passes. Of course, we couldn't get through the gate without a boarding pass. Whilst making our case at the gate, the captain of our plane appeared. Di grabbed him and explained the situation. He fixed it somehow and we were allowed to board. Once aboard, the hostess in charge brought us a bottle of champagne. 'I think you good people probably deserve this,' she said. We did and thanked her profusely. After two bad experiences, we have no plans to return to Mumbai, as it is now known, in a hurry.

Although we made various local trips during the remainder of the year, including visits to the Philippines, Bangkok and Macau, we could not justify the time to return to England that summer and I had a company conference to organize in Macau.

We derived enormous pleasure from our junk, which was licensed to carry up to about forty people, but we preferred to keep our parties small and rarely took out more than a dozen friends. Unlike many people, who liked to head for a seafood restaurant on one of the many islands, we enjoyed venturing out to secluded anchorages and entertaining on board, preparing all sorts of food, including chilli, curries, coronation chicken, new potatoes or rice and a wide variety of salads. This was followed by a dessert or fruit and cheese. Our meals on board were naturally washed down with copious quantities of wine – sometimes preceded by Bloody Marys,

Pimm's or champagne. A sundowner on the way home, watching the sun go down and listening to the susurration of the waves on the bow, made the perfect ending to a day out in the sun.

During the 1990s, we also started some serious hiking; partly because we were concerned about our level of fitness but also in anticipation of major expeditions to New Zealand that we were to undertake a few years later. Despite common misconceptions, Hong Kong has so much to offer the hiker: stunning scenery, mountains and country parks with numerous trails. We spent many a weekend walking the New Territories: Shing Mun, Plover Cove, Pat Sin Leng, Lam Tsuen, Tai Mo Shan, Tai Lam, Ma On Shan and Sai Kung – all country parks offering the hiker a very special experience.

In November of 1990, my parents moved to Lympstone in East Devon. My father had always intended to retire to Devon but just had not found the right property. Retirement to Hythe was a good compromise but Father yearned to return to Devon, his native county.

I should mention here my father's love of dogs, which was reignited in Lympstone. Abel, a Welsh border collie acquired by my father in 1976, sadly had to be put down in September 1990. In Lympstone, he came to know a neighbour's dog called Gemma, with whom he fast became friends. And then Lottie, a Jack Russell, came on the scene and she remained with my father until he could no longer cope and asked a friend to look after her.

In June 1991, we embarked on an adventure: we went to Shanghai by sea. Richard joined us. The ship, the name of which I forget, was Chinese and the only passenger vessel plying the route from Hong Kong to Shanghai. It was previously owned by an Antipodean shipping line and was now much in need of a refit. On the top deck, there was a derelict swimming pool surrounded by broken chairs.

The large saloon, perhaps grand in its heyday, was now run down and deserted. It was still home to an out-of-tune grand piano, which I attempted to play on one or two occasions. The entire trip was a hoot and much more fun than flying.

Knowing that the ship was not top-drawer, we had booked the most expensive suites nearest the bow of the ship. Having been warned about the quality of the meals on board, we also took vast quantities of food and drink to see us through the four-day voyage – cold boxes packed with cooked chicken, tomatoes and other perishables, as well as numerous cans and several wine boxes.

Having taken a tender out to the ship, which was moored on the eastern side of the harbour, we struggled up the ship's ladder. Apparently, in our excitement, Richard and I quickly scaled the ladder, leaving Di to bring up most of the supplies, assisted by the crew.

After boarding, we were escorted to our suites, which proved to be surprisingly comfortable. As we set sail, we ordered our first beers, headed for the deck and bade farewell to Hong Kong. Unfortunately, after several beers, it seemed that the ship ran out of stock – and this was only day one.

Interestingly, we did not head east out of the harbour through the Lei Yue Mun Channel, as one might expect. Instead, we sailed through the harbour, down the East Lamma Channel and around the south side of the island. I believe this was because the width and depth of Lei Yue Mun Channel were not adequate to ensure safe passage for large ships. In addition, because Lei Yue Mun lay below the flight path of Kai Tak Airport, ships whose masts or superstructures exceeded 100 feet above sea level could not enter or leave harbour through this channel unless fitted with VHF and permission had been obtained from Hong Kong Port Radio. Kai Tak Airport was closed in 1998 so this restriction no longer applies.

Once at sea, there was little to do or see as we were too far from the China coast, but we did spot several pods of whales breaching in the Taiwan Strait. However, we ate and drank well from our own larder. We took breakfast in the 'first-class' section of the ship's salon with one other couple. It was not a pleasant experience: inedible scrambled egg or congee, deep-fried dough sticks and soybean milk. On the second or third day, one of the waitresses asked me why we never came to the restaurant for lunch or dinner.

'You not eat?' she asked with some concern in her best Chinglish.

'Follow me,' I replied, and guided her to our suite.

She looked wide-eyed at the array of food sitting on the side table.

'Ah, I see you eat well,' she said with a broad smile.

Heading north-north-east up the coast of Zhejiang in the East China Sea, we were approaching Shanghai. On the fourth day, as dawn was breaking, we entered the estuary of the mighty Yangtze River. I had risen very early to prepare to video the first sight of Shanghai from the water. I went up on deck but, alas, the air was filled with fog and pollution. There was nothing to see.

In Shanghai, we stayed at the Peace Hotel (now the Fairmont Peace Hotel) on The Bund. The larger North Building, built in art deco style, was completed in the 1920s and is famous for the Old Jazz Band, recognized by Guinness World Records as the world's oldest, aka most elderly, jazz band, with an average age of eighty-two (in October 2019). The origins of the band date back to the 1940s. We spent many an evening with drinks and much dancing in the Jazz Bar.

We were joined at lunchtime on our first day by the rest of our Shanghai party who, unadventurously, had decided to travel by air. The other members of the group from Hong Kong included Angus Wilkinson, Winnie Whittaker, Irene O'Shea and Marilyn Hood, the three ladies now sadly dead. We usually met for pre-dinner drinks in our room as it was a suite with a sizeable sitting room. We had a ball.

We visited Pudong, almost opposite the Peace Hotel on the east side of the Huangpu River. It was a desert, originally farmland and still pretty much undeveloped. Two years later, in 1993, the Chinese government set up a Special Economic Zone, creating the Pudong New Area. Today, Pudong has become the financial hub of modern China and has several landmark buildings, including the Oriental Pearl Tower, the Jin Mao Building, Shanghai World Financial Center and Shanghai Tower. Pudong is also home to the Shanghai Stock Exchange and Shanghai Pudong International Airport. The transformation over a period of two decades has been astonishing. Most of the photographs of Shanghai you will see today showcase the glitzy financial district of Lujiazui in Pudong.

Di and I visited Lympstone for the first time in August 1991. We stopped over in Bahrain, where Robert had been posted after a stint back in London. He had a beautiful single-storey house with an enormous garden where we barbecued most days. When we arrived, we found gas masks placed on our bed. This was a partly humorous gesture but not entirely as the Gulf War had only been concluded a few months earlier.

The Gulf War came about when Iraqi dictator Saddam Hussein invaded neighbouring Kuwait in August 1990. The United Nations deadline for Iraqi forces to withdraw by 15th January 1991 was ignored, resulting in a US-led coalition force made up of nearly one million service personnel from thirty-two countries entering Kuwait, following an air war, and ousting Iraqi forces. The war was over within seven months.

The war marked the introduction of live news broadcasts from the front lines of the battle, principally by the US news network, CNN. I have vivid memories of sandwich lunches in Chesterton

Petty's boardroom in Jardine House, watching events unfold live. It was unsettling, frightening.

Besides the mandatory sightseeing in Bahrain, Di and I spent some time in the souks (Arab bazaars) buying gold jewellery. Robert also took us to a nightclub with belly dancers galore. I was still keen on using a video camera in those days and decided to film these extraordinary dancers. However, the manager had a quiet word, asking me to stop lest his regular high-net-worth patrons should later be identified with their mistresses. I understood entirely.

Di and I loved Lympstone and enjoyed seeing my parents apparently happy in their new home. My Aunty Bunty was living with my parents and Christopher joined us too. We spent many hours in the garden and celebrated my father's sixty-ninth birthday with a dinner at a nearby farmhouse where the owner hosted private dinners for paying guests.

It was during this visit that my mother suggested that we should get married. It has to be said that my mother had been obsessed with the idea of my marrying a 'nice girl' for as long as I can remember, but I do not recall her ever expressing her thoughts so seriously. We agreed, and we decided that we would arrange the marriage in Hong Kong later that year. No doubt, my parents would have liked to see us married in England – even in the lovely church in Lympstone – but it was simply not practicable.

On 8th November 1991, Di and I were married. We woke up to a beautiful morning in Greenery Garden with warm sunshine and a gentle breeze. Looking across the West Lamma Channel, the peaks of Lantau Island appeared as cardboard cut-outs on an azure sky.

We made preparations for the arrival of our two witnesses, Richard Gocher and Stephanie Latham, who had been a good friend since our return to Hong Kong in 1988. We were all members of our CCC Club, which the four of us had set up to enjoy the game of canasta along with champagne and caviar (the three Cs), rotating once a month between our homes. Robert, who was not sure that he would be able to come to the ceremony at all because of his demanding travel schedule, was in the end able to attend and joined us for lunch.

Not surprisingly, we celebrated with champagne and caviar at lunchtime before making our way to the Cotton Tree Drive Marriage Registry in Hong Kong Park. As was the case in my first marriage, we could not be married in church because I was a divorcee.

We asked John Chynchen, a friend and Honorary Chaplain of St John's Cathedral (and incidentally, like me, a chartered surveyor), if he would give us a marriage blessing in the cathedral. He agreed, of course, but pointed out that the cathedral was in the midst of a major renovation. He suggested that we hold the blessing in St Stephen's Chapel in Stanley, a daughter church of St John's Cathedral.

The chapel forms part of St Stephen's College, founded in 1903 and relocated to Stanley in 1928. However, the chapel itself was not built until after the Second World War and was consecrated in 1950. During the war, the college became a military hospital but, on Christmas Day 1941, the invading Japanese troops stormed the college, killing up to sixty wounded soldiers as well as doctors and nurses. Following the British surrender, St Stephen's became an internment camp until the war ended in 1945.

The stained-glass memorial window in the chapel is a poignant reminder of the past, but, despite the memories, the chapel is in a beautiful setting, modest in design, and we agreed to John's suggestion immediately.

We decided to keep the ceremony very small and invited just a few guests: Richard and Stephanie, our witnesses, along with Robert, Hanifa, my assistant, Michael and Jean Dalton and Wendy Glynn. John Chynchen conducted the ceremony beautifully. Both Robert and Michael Dalton gave a reading. Following the service, there was a photography session, of course.

Early that evening, we held a formal reception in the Hong Kong Club to which we invited sixty or seventy guests for drinks and canapés. The party lasted several hours, following which Robert had arranged to take six of us to dinner at Amigo, a French restaurant in Happy Valley. Amigo was one of the best restaurants in Hong Kong but Di and I were so exhausted by the time the first course was served at around 9.00 pm that we could hardly keep our eyes open. Nonetheless, it was a very special day.

Di and I had set up a wedding list at Town House, a shop selling glass and silver in Prince's Building in Central. We wanted to collect a set of Waterford Lismore crystal glass. We did very well by so many friends and colleagues and now have a large collection of Waterford crystal, rarely used these days because it is rather out of fashion.

My co-directors at Chesterton Petty gave us a very special present: Business Class flights and two nights at the Manila Hotel, a five-star hotel on Manila Bay in the Philippines. This mini-honeymoon gave us a much-needed rest and we enjoyed it enormously.

I must also mention the amusing story of a special present of a make-up session given to Di by Lindy Jackman and her husband, Sam, friends from New Zealand based in Hong Kong. Di set off on the morning of our wedding day, excited at the prospect of her 'new' face. However, she returned before lunch, almost in tears. She looked like a Japanese geisha with pallid make-up plastered all over her face. We all agreed that she should remove her make-up entirely and start from scratch. This is what she did and we all then enjoyed a glass of champagne. When Lindy arrived at the reception, dressed up to the nines, she tilted Di's wide-brimmed hat up a little and said, 'My goodness, that make-up didn't last long, did it?' She never knew the truth.

My mother died on 23rd May 1992. I had not seen her since our visit to Lympstone in August 1991. My father telephoned me in the middle of the afternoon while Di and I were having a rest and told me she had suffered a heart attack while making early-morning tea in the kitchen. I was close to my mother and this completely unexpected news shocked me deeply. I was terribly distraught.

It was a Saturday and we were expected at Richard's flat in the evening for our regular CCC Club dinner with Stephanie. Given the circumstances, I knew that I would not be up to it. However, Di looked after me and a few hours later we talked and decided that perhaps going out would take my mind off this sad news. I was very subdued during the evening, while Richard calmed me with brandy, but it probably was the best thing I could have done.

I recall we had arranged a junk trip the next day. I was once again very downcast but going out and meeting friends took my mind off the reality that my mother was gone forever.

My father told me some months later that the doctor had misdiagnosed the cause of my mother's death. He explained that the condition of my mother immediately after her death did not indicate a heart attack and he asked for a post-mortem. I was rather shocked and upset to learn that the cause of death was actually asphyxia through food inhalation. My mother had always had oesophageal problems and a tendency to choke on her food – and this is clearly what happened that morning.

One of the saddest aspects of her death for me was that, although she knew that Di and I were married, she never had the opportunity to see us as a married couple. She would have relished this moment, which would have made her very happy. *C'est la vie.*

Di and I returned to Lympstone for the funeral service, which my father conducted in the parish church on 29th May. After the service, friends and relations gathered in the garden on a beautiful sunny day for the wake. My mother was cremated at the Devon and Exeter Crematorium and her ashes placed in Lympstone churchyard.

Elaine and Sarah came to the funeral and I suggested that

Sarah should visit me in Hong Kong. This was agreed and she came out in the summer. Di and I met her off the plane, accompanied by a British Airways 'flying nanny' (a service that BA ended in January 2017) and we drove back to Greenery Garden.

Sarah had a marvellous time. We took her to many places around Hong Kong, including an overnight visit to Beas River Country Club, where we enjoyed the facilities as part of our membership of the Royal Hong Kong Jockey Club, and Ocean Park. Since Di was working and I was not willing to go on the roller coaster and most of the other rides at Ocean Park, I had to cajole some friends, Russell and Shirley Davie, to come with me. They were brilliant and gave Sarah the time of her life. We had the junk too, of course, which she loved. We visited many of the outlying islands, including Lamma Island where we often visited the 'pigeon restaurant' which, as you might expect, served fat meaty pigeons, deep-fried with crispy skin. It was a highly successful visit and gave us all the opportunity to spend time together.

On 1st October 1992, aged forty-two, I gave up smoking. I had tried unsuccessfully before and knew that the time had come. Both my parents smoked but my first experience was at Marlborough, buying my Player's N°6 and setting off on my bike for a secret smoke in the countryside. I seriously doubted whether I would succeed in giving up, having seen so many people fail, but I mentally prepared myself and bought nicotine patches to help me along. It was easier than I expected and I was able to wean myself off the patches within two or three months. Despite some temptations in the early days, particularly where alcohol was involved, I am proud to say that I have never had a single puff since giving up.

My father visited us in November 1992. For all the years I had been in Hong Kong, he appeared reluctant to come and see me. And then he decided to come. Perhaps there was a fear of the long-haul flight – he had never flown except for a short flight during the war – but I suspect the reality was that he just didn't want to come with my mother.

Our home in Greenery Garden was perfect for him. He used to sit on the balcony observing the passing ships; the sea had always been close to his heart. Apart from the usual tourist runs, we introduced him to many of our friends and we all enjoyed drinks and dinners in the Foreign Correspondents' Club, the Royal Hong Kong Yacht Club and elsewhere. Like Sarah, he loved going out on our boat – being at sea. We also took him to Shelter Cove, the Yacht Club's 'country club' way up in the New Territories; and on several occasions, he and I took the Aberdeen Boat Club's tender to Middle Island, another Yacht Club outlet. I would buy us each a large whisky in the Boat Club's bar and we would enjoy a pre-prandial drink while motoring to Middle Island.

Di and I were planning to celebrate our first wedding anniversary – when guests traditionally give paper presents – with a black-tie dinner for sixteen people at the Royal Hong Kong Yacht Club, a tradition which we maintained for several years. I had asked Father to bring a dinner jacket for the occasion, which he was not very happy about, but nonetheless he enjoyed this special evening and meeting some of our friends, despite being unexpectedly cajoled into giving an after-dinner speech.

It was at this dinner that I introduced my father to Jenny Thomas, who worked with me in Richard Ellis's Kowloon office in 1984-85, and her husband, Roger, who proposed the toast. Jenny invited Father to their home in Clear Water Bay. They seemed to get on rather well – and my father certainly took a shine to her.

A few days later, I arranged for one of our company drivers to take Father in my car to Clear Water Bay – I think he was rather impressed by the luxury car and chauffeur service! Jenny drove my father with her mother and stepfather to Sai Kung East Country Park before taking the ferry to Tap Mun, a small island about forty minutes by ferry from Wong Shek Pier, where they had lunch in Mr Loi's Seafood Restaurant, a very 'local' Chinese restaurant owned by two young graduates of Manchester University.

'How was your day?' I asked my father when he got home.

'Super day. Jenny was delightful. I had no idea the countryside parks were so beautiful, with mountains sweeping down to the sea, splendid views and reminiscent of the Western Isles.'

'I don't think many people realize how beautiful the New Territories are. They think of Hong Kong as a concrete jungle, which is far from the truth. Did Jenny take you to Tap Mun, as she mentioned the other night?'

'Yes. Lovely ferry trip but I ate hardly anything as it was all prawns, squid and other seafood. Not my scene at all.'

'Oh dear.'

'We walked up a hill behind the village and watched the rollers coming in from the South China Sea. It reminded me of the Cornish coast. But the village itself was extraordinary: shanties, broken-down shops and a narrow, evil-smelling main street.'

'That's Hong Kong, I'm afraid. The Chinese often seem to have no pride in their environment. You can see discarded fridges, broken bikes and all sorts of detritus all around the villages. It's so sad when you think of the beautiful surroundings.'

My father loved his time with us in Hong Kong and promised to return the following year in October, when the weather would be a little warmer with temperatures around twenty-five degrees Celsius, a few degrees warmer than in November.

For some reason, we visited Mr Loi's Seafood Restaurant on Tap Mun again. However, on this occasion, he ate sandwiches which we prepared at home while Di and I tucked into the local fare. I am not sure what the owners made of my father's eating habits; I think they looked on with benign amusement.

*

Di and I have a tradition of celebrating Christmas at home. Over the years, we have invited many friends home to enjoy a formal sit-down Christmas lunch or dinner with all the trimmings – and far too many presents. We are usually eight in number but, on one occasion, I had to buy a folding table top which sat on top of our usual table and allowed ten of us to sit down comfortably.

In 1992, however, Richard invited us to join him for Christmas in the villa he owned with his sister, Sue, in Bordeaux. He had also asked four other friends: Mark and Julie Summerville, who now live in Sydney, and two other friends from England, Robin and Lizzie. It was a classic French villa, built in attractive grey stone, with a garden and overlooking fields of vines.

The weather was chilly, as expected, and there was a dusting of snow on some days, but we all cosied up in front of a log fire and thoroughly enjoyed ourselves. Julie decorated the Christmas tree beautifully and we agreed a rota for cooking and washing-up.

Di and I were assigned to cook on Christmas Eve and we decided to make a boeuf bourguignon. We found a heavy cast-iron pan, which was ideal for the job. Having browned the beef and softened the onions, we added the red wine and other ingredients. However, after half an hour or so of gently simmering the meat, we noticed brown speckles in the sauce. We investigated and finally poured the entire contents of the pan into another vessel. We quickly discovered that the cast-iron pan was rusting – probably the result of many years of disuse. After a brief panic, we decided to drain off the sauce and thoroughly rinse the remaining ingredients. We then made a new sauce in a different pan. We did not say a word to the assembled guests and everybody thoroughly enjoyed a superb Christmas Eve dinner!

Our Christmas meal was very much a joint effort. Robin and Lizzie had brought the turkey from England as it was not possible to buy a decent bird in France. Each of us was responsible for particular duties, although I have no recollection of my personal role. There is apparently a photograph of Richard and me icing the Christmas cake.

One day, Richard took us to the Restaurant Francis Goullée, a classic French restaurant in Saint-Émilion, a beautiful medieval village, apparently named after a monk who fled from Brittany and evangelized the local people. In 1999, the Jurisdiction of Saint-Émilion, which includes eight surrounding villages and a 'historic vineyard landscape', was inscribed on UNESCO's World Heritage List.

The lunch was a very grand affair, with *amuse-bouches* and three courses to follow, accompanied by fine clarets and a little cognac to finish. As a well-known French restaurant, it was not surprising to find that the cuisine was incredibly rich and Richard most certainly suffered. I enjoyed it.

After a very special Christmas, Di and I spent the New Year in Paris, where we stayed in a boutique hotel close to the centre for two or three nights. Our first task was to find a suitable restaurant in which to celebrate the New Year – or La Saint-Sylvestre as the French call it. It was very cold and trudging around the streets was not a great pleasure. Finding a restaurant proved quite a challenge as most restaurants were either fully booked or offering a highly expensive table d'hôte dinner. We finally came across the ideal venue: a small Italian restaurant, run by a *mamma* and *papà* couple, who were offering the perfect dinner at a sensible price.

I think we were one of a very few couples who actually received the full dinner. Guests who arrived later were complaining of the long wait to be served and the absence of roast potatoes. Diners were becoming agitated and there was even a scuffle with the chef outside on the street. At this point, several diners simply walked out – without paying. The owners' children were crying. It was chaos. Di and I went to look after the children while the owners tried to calm the few remaining guests. This was not a happy night.

After matters settled down, we enjoyed a drink with the owners and finally paid our bill. We left before midnight. Just to add to the evening's misfortunes, it appeared that my credit card was out of date and wouldn't work. I promised to sort it out and we returned the following day to pay our bill. We did not stay for a meal. The owners were enormously grateful for our honesty.

When we arrived back at our hotel after dinner, we turned on the television news and were shocked to discover that there had been a New Year's Eve tragedy in Lan Kwai Fong, one of Hong Kong's most popular bar districts, particularly for expatriates. By now, it was morning time in Hong Kong.

The story in the *South China Morning Post* read: 'Up to twenty people were reported to have been killed and more than 100 injured in a stampede involving some of the 20,000 in Lan Kwai Fong in Central for New Year celebrations last night. The crush occurred when people surged out into the streets from the district's restaurants and bars as the countdown to midnight was being broadcast on TVB.' At the scene, 'a large number of people were shocked and dazed and a lot of them were crying'. The eventual death toll was confirmed at twenty-one.

We had a sleepless night; not only because we were shocked by the news but also because the young people of Paris appeared hell-bent on shouting drunkenly throughout the night. We have never been devotees of New Year's Eve but this was the last straw.

Chapter 9

Uncharted Waters

1993-1997

Our second lease at Greenery Gardens came to an end in February 1993. I had approached the landlord about buying the property but simply could not afford to do so without selling my flat in Richmond, which I was not prepared to do. So we started the search for a new property and entered into a lease in Vienna Court, Realty Gardens, where we stayed for almost ten years.

Realty Gardens in Mid-Levels was built in the early 1970s and is situated almost halfway up Victoria Peak, about twenty minutes' walk from Central District. It is famous not only as the original location of the Foreign Correspondents' Club but also as the hospital in the 1955 film, *Love is a Many-Splendored Thing*. Many of the balustrades where William Holden and Jennifer Jones conducted their fairy-tale romance are still visible today.

Our new flat looked into the hillside and was about the same size as Greenery Garden but did not have the spectacular view or the light. We looked across to the swimming pool but, because the pool was at the same elevation as our seventh-floor flat, we could not see very much. Nonetheless, it was a good flat in a very convenient location in Mid-Levels and we enjoyed our time there.

In the spring of 1993, I had the opportunity to participate in a training course and become an Associate of the Chartered Institute of Arbitrators, a highly respected body set up in 1915 to mediate and resolve disputes and thereby avoid costly court proceedings. Following completion of the course, I duly sat the exams and passed. I cannot say that I ever made use of this qualification but it was adding another string to my bow and I always enjoyed the challenge of learning. (In 1991, I had become a Fellow of the Hong Kong Institute of Surveyors, although no exams were involved as I had already qualified as a chartered surveyor in the UK.)

I wanted to take Di to Bali, having visited on my own ten years before. In July, we hired a jeep and toured the island, which I had not seen since I only spent a couple of nights in Sanur in 1983. It was pure magic. Di loved every part of this tropical, volcanic island; home to beautiful beaches, rice fields, Hindu temples and a gentle, colourful people with whom one could somehow relate. We drove around the island, visiting Ubud, the arty centre, and ending in Sanur on the east coast. We have stayed in Sanur at least ten times since, often travelling with friends, exploring new parts of the island and simply soaking up the relaxed, almost spiritual atmosphere that pervades the island. Bali remains one of our favourite destinations, although these days we tend to travel very little and just relax in our hotel.

I returned from our trip to Bali in 1993 with some apprehension. There had been some issues in the company, the outcome of which was that the managing director had stepped down. We would need to appoint a replacement. George Doran, who was due to retire and had stepped in as acting managing director, advised me that the situation could be difficult for me since the prime candidate for the position was the director who had little time for me. However, after much discussion among the directors, the position was taken up by Gordon Moffoot, who had always supported me. He was appointed managing director some months later and remained in post until August 2005.

My father returned to see us, as promised, in October 1993. He was seventy-one. Once again, we gave him a marvellous time but I know he missed the spectacular view we had enjoyed at Greenery Gardens. We spent time on the junk and also stayed in a somewhat primitive Price Waterhouse weekend retreat in the north-east New Territories.

Early on, my friend Richard invited us all to a cocktail party at his apartment in Blue Pool Road, Happy Valley. At this party, my father met Julie Petersen, who had just landed a job in Hong Kong and was staying with Richard until she settled down and found her own accommodation. I think they both took a shine to each other and, if my memory serves me correctly, there was a good deal of flirtation – certainly from Father, if not Julie.

We also took him to Beas River Country Club in the New Territories. The club is set in beautiful surroundings adjoining the Hong Kong Golf Club's Fanling course and with views of Lam Tsuen Country Park and the Pat Sin Leng mountain range. Shenzhen, China's southernmost metropolis with a population of over twelve million, is just eight kilometres north as the crow flies; and yet the club is an oasis of tranquility, away from the constant hustle and bustle of the city, with an equestrian centre that includes a world-class riding school and a livery of retired racehorses. It is a very peaceful and relaxing setting.

Di had recently had a minor operation on her foot, which started bleeding profusely while she was at the poolside. I went off to look for help and came across the club's nursing centre.

'Hi, I don't know whether you can help me. My wife has recently had an operation on the sole of her foot and it's started bleeding quite badly,' I explained to the resident nurse.

'I'm sure we can help. You know, humans are pretty much the same as horses when it comes to treating wounds,' she quipped.

I wondered if they only treated horses. She bandaged Di's foot beautifully.

Later that year, Di went on a business trip to Beijing.* Richard and I decided to take the opportunity to go too; neither of us had ever been to Beijing. We stayed in the grand five-star China World Hotel, adjoining the China World Trade Center and situated in the city's imposing Chaoyang District.

Beijing is a sprawling city and is steeped in history dating back three millennia. We visited the Forbidden City, Tiananmen Square, the Temple of Heaven, the Great Wall and the Summer Palace as well as walking for many miles through the city's historic streets, including the famous *hutongs*, centuries-old narrow twisting alleys. The sheer scale and grandeur of these structures is breathtaking. So many ancient buildings in China are painted in vermilion red, the colour of fire and blood, with yellow-tiled roofs, an imperial colour associated with emperors.

There was a distinct chill in the air, sooty skies and a dusting of snow heralding the approach of winter descending upon the city. One lasting memory is the vast piles of cabbages for sale on every street

---

* *The Chinese capital did not change its name from Peking to Beijing, as many people think. Peking was simply the older transliteration of the Chinese characters meaning 'Northern Capital' before the pinyin romanization system was introduced by the Chinese government in the 1950s. However, it was not until the 1980s that the use of the name Beijing became widespread and adopted by international bodies.*

corner, a sure sign that Beijingers would not starve. The tradition of hoarding dates back to the 1950s when hunger was commonplace as food was scarce under the communist regime. However, the winter stockpiling has long gone following the introduction of new farming practices, making supplies more plentiful.

We spent Christmas 1993 at home. Sarah came to stay with us again. Philip and Niki Goodstein were in Hong Kong and Richard joined us too. Di and I prepared lunch for the six of us and I recall there was a lengthy game of Monopoly afterwards, which had to be brought to a close, despite Sarah's protestations. Shortly after Christmas, we took Sarah to Boracay in the Philippines, flying from Manila to the island in a six-seater plane, much to Sarah's delight.

Since returning to Hong Kong in 1988, I had been increasingly concerned about a pension. In England, a company pension was very much the norm in those days, but in Hong Kong few companies offered similar benefits other than major corporations. Some companies provided a provident fund, which is a form of saving, a lump sum being paid to the employee on retirement or resignation. Chesterton Petty provided no such benefits at the time, although the Hong Kong Government set up the Mandatory Provident Fund scheme in 2000.

Given that I was now forty-four years of age, I knew I needed to make some provision for later life. I prepared a business plan for investing in residential property in university cities in the UK and set up a tax-efficient offshore company in the British Virgin Islands, Cygnet International Ltd, to hold the assets. Several friends showed interest in investing and, in the end, Richard Gocher joined me as an equal shareholder.

Our first property, a two-bedroom flat, was bought off-plan in a new development in the centre of Oxford. This was followed by properties in Cambridge, Bristol, Brighton and Nottingham. A second company, Regalis International Ltd, was established, but company purchases were put on hold at this stage owing to lack of investment funds. However, Di and I decided to buy in our own names and we acquired several properties in Hong Kong and the UK, including a flat in Coin Street near the National Theatre on London's South Bank.

Monitoring the property market very carefully, I suggested to Richard that we 'sell all' as the market approached its peak in 2007. He agreed and we began to divest ourselves of our holdings. Di and I did likewise, although the sale of my flat in Richmond, which I had bought in 1983, was delayed for several months because of problems with the tenant. It has to be said that my timing was perfect and this venture was highly successful, enabling me to invest further in Hong Kong.

In May 1994, I came home one evening to find a letter from Elaine, my former wife, announcing that Sarah would be coming to live with Di and me in the summer for the foreseeable future. I was somewhat taken aback, to put it mildly. This missive came completely out of the blue. I poured myself a large drink, sat down and started thinking through all the implications.

It transpired that Elaine was in a very difficult relationship with an extremely jealous man and poor Sarah bore the brunt of this. I know that Sarah was feeling very dejected at this time and, although she was worried about going to school in Hong Kong and missing her friends, I believe Elaine's decision was for the best. Sadly, Sarah was not really old enough for her mother to explain why she had changed and was shutting Sarah out of her life. In any event, it was clear that Elaine had decided it was my turn to take over, which I was very happy to do – albeit with some trepidation.

When Di returned from the office, we discussed the situation. She seemed more relaxed about it than I did but, honestly speaking,

I don't think she realized how life would change with a thirteen-year-old stepdaughter in tow. Notwithstanding, we embraced the idea and immediately starting thinking about schooling. Notice was very short as term would start at the end of August, but we were very fortunate in securing a place for Sarah at Island School, a private international school within the English Schools Foundation. Today, one would have little hope of finding a place at such short notice. We transformed our spare bedroom, switching the double bed for a single and making other changes to prepare for Sarah's arrival.

I well remember the extraordinary day we collected Sarah in August. Elaine did not want us to pick up Sarah from her home, as we would have expected; we were to meet in the village square in Faringdon. When we crossed the square and approached Elaine's car, a forlorn Sarah got out with her bag and hockey stick. As I was about to speak to Elaine, she drove off with her then boyfriend – without a single word. Sarah was terribly upset, of course, but she started to calm down as we drove away. We stayed the night with our friends outside Bristol, Jenny and David Peers, whose children were very good with Sarah, before we drove to stay with my father in Lympstone. Elaine recently explained to me that her boyfriend had not allowed her to speak to me – nor even make eye contact.

Sarah had written to me before she came to Hong Kong with some concerns, one question being whether the school bus driver would be Chinese. This always amused me. She need not have worried; she settled into her new life in Hong Kong very quickly. She made some good friends, including her first 'proper' boyfriend (as far as we knew), some of whom she still keeps in touch with.

This was not an easy time but I think we all fared well. Di and I had no experience of parenting a teenager. Di often says that she did not do well by Sarah and was not perhaps the 'mother' she would like to have been. This is far from the truth. She was wonderful with Sarah and I could never have managed without her wisdom and support. I was far too soft, of course, and it was Di who had to put her foot down about all sorts of issues. There was one occasion when Sarah announced that she and others would be going for a sleepover at a boy's house. Di asked her if the parents would be present and it seemed that they would almost certainly not be there. We banned the sleepover, much to Sarah's chagrin. We found out a short time later that the sleepover never took place because the other parents had also banned their children from going.

Sarah went home to England for the summer holidays in 1995 and 1996. This seemed to work well, despite the difficulties at Mother's home. Elaine obviously missed her and it gave them valuable time to mend fences. Christmases were spent with us in Hong Kong, other than in 1996 when Di and I were in New Zealand.

The three years that Sarah spent living with us in Hong Kong were invaluable for all of us. I know she appreciated the opportunities given to her, which broadened her perspective on life.

'We became a family unit in our own right and grew far closer than would have been possible had I not come,' she told me not long ago. 'I feel very lucky to have spent that time together and hugely value the relationship that I have with you and Di. My time living with you in Hong Kong built bridges in a way that only seeing you once or twice a year might not have done.'

After all, I left England before Sarah reached her fourth birthday and only saw her on my annual visits home.

Sarah's words mean so much to me and reflect my own feelings, which have perhaps remained unsaid.

I had also started learning Mandarin Chinese, the official language of mainland China. With Hong Kong reverting to China in 1997 and Chesterton planning to expand into China, I felt this would be useful. I loved Mandarin as a language, with its sing-song tones, and I wanted the challenge. I enjoyed it – learning to read and write as well as speak. I particularly enjoyed writing – or more often than not typing – the characters. However, it was an expensive and time-consuming occupation, particularly the written homework which might involve several hours to produce a few paragraphs. I decided to give it up after a year or two, a decision I regret because, by now, I would hopefully be a competent Mandarin speaker.

Chesterton Petty established a new Kowloon office in Harbour City in 1994. The business was expanding, staff numbers were on the rise and space was running out. It was agreed that I would run the office, which included the Kowloon agency teams and our Building Consultancy Division as well as the Property Management Division, which was moving back to Kowloon. By this time, Hanifa, my former marketing assistant, had transferred to the Commercial Agency Department and Linda, who was her assistant, took up her position in marketing. Justiner, one of the most important cogs in the property-management machine, worked alongside me. I was still running the Research and Marketing Division, so was wearing several hats.

Besides my marketing and research responsibilities, my focus was on developing and expanding the property-management business. This was not an easy task since the majority of owners' corporations were run by Chinese and there were usually language problems, with many owners' meetings being conducted primarily in Cantonese. I recall one meeting where the owners refused to speak in English and I sat rather like a miserable wallflower at a boisterous party. I think I probably excused myself to make a point. I knew that the task would best be handled by experienced Chinese property managers and I therefore delegated much of the responsibility to my managers. I held regular meetings with the managers and staff, most of whom spoke excellent English.

At this time, I was president of the Hong Kong Association of

Property Management Companies. As director in charge of property management at Chesterton, I had been invited to join the association two years before and was elected president in 1994 – a position that I reluctantly accepted. Given the nature of property management in Hong Kong, I felt that the position should be held by a Chinese member and that I was not sufficiently experienced in this field. Nonetheless, there was an overwhelming vote for me; perhaps because I displayed the leadership skills required and I presented very well. I was the first president ever to serve two years. Ironically, however, there was a coup at the next AGM and the few expatriate members of the governing council were voted off. Frankly, I was relieved.

As president, I led council members of the association on a number of trips, including to Beijing, where we met all sorts of government officials who spoke little or no English. One of my colleagues therefore had to act as translator. At one of the official dinners at which I had to give a speech, I decided to speak in Mandarin. Rather than trying to keep it very simple, I attempted to translate an English idiom into Mandarin while I watched the members of my audience looking increasingly perplexed. Of course, I had been far too ambitious in thinking I could succeed at my very modest linguistic level in what is a notoriously difficult language to master, especially when it comes to the tones. A mistake. However, the audience appreciated my attempt – even if they hadn't understood a word – and clapped enthusiastically.

Chesterton Petty set up an office in Shanghai in 1995, the main purpose being to manage a large commercial complex which had recently been completed by a developer client. As the director in charge, I went to Shanghai along with a Chinese colleague for the grand opening. It was an accolade for Chesterton to have won this business and was the turning point for the company in China. We opened an office in Beijing shortly afterwards.

Around this time, I was approached by the managing director

of a leading property consultancy in Hong Kong. He wanted me to take up a position, based in the Philippines, involved with the planning and management of Fort Bonifacio, a major new urban development in Manila. Despite numerous discussions and a trip to Manila, this job did not work out. It was clear that the local American boss only wanted to employ an American. In the event, it was just as well because it would have caused a serious upset with Sarah's schooling in the middle of her GCSEs.

In 1995, Richard suggested that we should all visit South Africa, where he had worked for many years in the 1970s. He had friends, Brian and Jane Aslett, who lived in Johannesburg and agreed to join us on a trip to Cape Town, Stellenbosch and Cape Winelands.

We flew to Johannesburg with Air Mauritius. At the time, Richard was working on the Air Mauritius advertising account and was able to secure us an upgrade. We stayed for a night or two in Sandton, one of the safest areas of the city. However, hearing that most residents kept a gun by their bedside did not help to make us feel very comfortable. We were glad to escape to Cape Town, which is an attractive city on the south-west coast beneath the imposing Table Mountain. We felt a great deal more comfortable walking around this city, although we were always 'looking over our shoulders', so to speak.

The five of us set off by car for Stellenbosch, a charming university town surrounded by mountains and vineyards. The town's oak-shaded streets were lined with cafés, boutiques and art galleries, and the Cape Dutch architecture reflected the country's colonial past. We ate and drank very well.

South Africa's townships, slum areas reserved for non-whites, have long been a blight on South Africa's history and still exist today, despite the end of apartheid more than twenty-five years ago. They are notoriously dangerous places. On one occasion, we took a wrong road and found ourselves driving through a township area. Richard was driving at the time and we were approaching traffic lights as they were turning red.

'Do not stop, Richard. Drive through the red light and keep driving,' said Brian.

We were all rather alarmed as carjacking was commonplace. We lived to tell the tale.

On our way back to Hong Kong, we stopped for a few days in Mauritius, an island nation in the Indian Ocean best known for its beautiful beaches and reefs. We did not find a great deal to see in the interior, other than endless fields of sugar cane, and foolishly we did not visit the Black River Gorges National Park in the south-west, which might have given us a different perspective. We spent a good deal of time at the Grand Bay Yacht Club, which I was able to access through my membership of the Royal Hong Kong Yacht Club.

I made a trip to Mauritius in 2005 on business at the request of two friends, Jonathan Shaw and Gordon Fisher, who lived and worked in Port Louis, the capital. They were looking at the feasibility of a potential residential development and sought my advice.

And in 2015, Di and I went to stay with Jonathan in his beautiful house in Roche Terre in the north-east of the island. Once again, we spent time at the Grand Bay Yacht Club, just twenty minutes' drive away, as well as exploring parts of the island hitherto unseen.

In my study in Barnes, I have two large photographs hanging over my desk, both taken from exactly the same spot at the Yacht Club: the first taken in 1995, the second in 2015. Nothing had changed.

Di and I were concerned about Sarah continuing her education in Hong Kong after the handover in 1997. Nobody really knew how the new regime would affect the education system – or indeed everyday life as we knew it; it was all an unknown quantity. We discussed with Sarah her going to boarding school in England for her A levels. She was planning to study biology, chemistry and maths, which would enable her to read medicine at university. She was very receptive to the idea, and I think she was also ready to slot back into life in England and with her mother.

In the summer of 1996, Di and I spent two weeks visiting private schools which we felt would be suitable. One criterion, requested by Elaine, was that the school should be within easy driving distance of her home in Gloucestershire; this made very good sense to us. We looked at quite a number of schools, including Warminster School, St Mary's School in Oxford (for which Sarah had to sit an exam in Hong Kong) and Bruton School for Girls. Our last port of call was Wells Cathedral School, where we were able to meet the headmaster, John Baxter. Our decision was made easy after a tour of the school and meeting this fine man. Sarah would start at Wells Cathedral School in the autumn term of 1997. Rightly or wrongly, Sarah had no real involvement in this exercise, which I suppose would not be the case today, when children would expect to visit the schools and be part of the decision-making process. However, she seemed very happy with the decision.

Sarah had spent three years with us in Hong Kong. She was very privileged, not only to attend one of the best private schools in Hong Kong, with consistently outstanding exam results, but also to experience a new culture and lifestyle. She also travelled with us to the Philippines, Bangkok and Bali. She grew up very quickly.

We made our first visit to New Zealand at Christmas in 1996. Once again, Richard joined us. We had been invited to spend Christmas Day with David and Stephanie Dignan, mutual friends from Hong Kong who now lived in Torbay on the city's North Shore. Richard had also arranged our accommodation in Sam and Lindy Jackman's house in St Heliers, a fashionable district on the east side of Auckland. Sam and Lindy, now living back in New Zealand, had driven north to the Bay of Islands so we had the house to ourselves. We stayed at least one night with David and Stephanie because we attended a candlelit Christmas Eve service at St Mary by the Sea Church, just a few minutes' walk from their house.

After Christmas, we hired a car and drove south to Rotorua and Lake Taipo, from where we explored the area. Rotorua is extraordinary. Sitting within the volcanic Pacific Rim of Fire, the area has one of the world's most active geothermal fields. We walked across moonlike landscapes with geysers erupting thirty metres into the air, hot bubbling mud pools, clouds of steam, colourful lakes and the unforgettable smell of sulphur.

We returned to Auckland and Richard flew to see friends in Melbourne. Di and I drove to the Bay of Islands, which is a good three hours north of Auckland. The weather was appalling and deteriorated as we headed north. Not far from Paihia, where we were staying, the road was closed due to flooding. We had to go back some considerable distance to Whangarei and take a different route, so the entire journey took us much longer than expected. We stayed in a motel, which was not very special, but everywhere else was fully booked.

The Bay of Islands is stunning, made up of more than 140 islands – a paradise for yachting and big-game fishing. It is also home to the charming nineteenth-century port of Russell, the country's first European settlement and seaport. The Waitangi Treaty Grounds, a short distance from Paihia, is an important historic site where, in 1840, New Zealand's founding document was signed.

Quite by chance, friends of ours who were living in Wellington on a UK Foreign Office posting, were also in the Bay of Islands. We were all invited by Sam and Lindy to a New Year's Eve barbecue. Although we all enjoyed a fun evening, it was evident that their marriage was in trouble and that Lindy was not a happy person.

Having taken a taxi home – queuing for a compulsory breath

test for all drivers on the way – we had a sleepless night with the constant sound of drunken youths roaming the town. The door to our room, which opened directly onto the motel grounds, was even rattled on a few occasions. There were many more youths around than normal as there was supposed to be a concert, cancelled because of the rains.

The following morning, with a suitable New Year's Day hangover, we went for a walk through a nearby forest, occasionally coming across intoxicated young people. It was a beautiful but not very comfortable walk.

We headed back to Auckland and home to Hong Kong. We were so taken with New Zealand – even on our first brief visit to the North Island – that we would return many times in the years to come.

In May 1997, I visited Xi'an, the capital of China's Shaanxi Province, in order to see the world-famous Terracotta Warriors. I went with Richard, Angus (who came with us to Shanghai) and Barbara (now his wife), and Gerry and Sheona Muttrie, friends from Hong Kong who now live in Edinburgh and Italy.

Xi'an is one of the oldest cities in China and is situated at the eastern end of the Silk Road. The Terracotta Warriors, life-size terracotta sculptures, depict the armies of the first Emperor of China and date from more than 2,200 years ago. There are some 8,000 sculptures, discovered underground by local farmers in 1974, which make for a truly phenomenal sight.

Following our visit to Xi'an, we flew to Beijing where we met up with Di, who had been on a business trip with Price Waterhouse. Having visited the Summer Palace in 1993, our main focus was the Old Summer Palace, which dates from 1709. In 1860, the British burned down the palace on the orders of Lord Elgin, the British High Commissioner to China, apparently in retaliation for the torture and killing of two British envoys. The present-day park is a collection of crumbling walls and ruins.

We organized a picnic lunch and sat amongst the ruins enjoying a fine spread of cold foods, washed down with plenty of wine. One of my most vivid memories is of Gerry, who has a wry sense of humour, adopting his 'Asian squat' while pretending to smoke. In the background was the countdown clock, which indicated the days, hours and minutes until the handover of Hong Kong to China at midnight on the evening of 30th June.

As I write these words, I can't help wondering if readers may be forgiven for assuming that we spend most of our time partying or on holiday. But the old adage, 'work hard, play hard', is true and it certainly seemed to apply to expatriates in Hong Kong. We have enjoyed many opportunities to travel but we have always worked hard.

Chapter 10

The Handover and Beyond

1997-2005

At midnight on the morning of 1st July 1997, the Crown Colony of Hong Kong officially reverted to Chinese sovereignty, ending 156 years of British rule. After the formal handover ceremony on the night of 30th June, the colony became the Hong Kong Special Administrative Region (HKSAR) of the People's Republic of China.

The Sino-British Joint Declaration, signed in December 1984, stipulated that under Chinese rule the Special Administrative Region would enjoy a high degree of autonomy, except in matters of foreign relations and defence, and that the social and economic systems as well as the lifestyle in Hong Kong would remain unchanged for fifty years after 1997. Many observers, however, expressed scepticism over China's pledge to abide by the 'One Country, Two Systems' principle.

There was a splendid handover party in the Hong Kong Club, which sadly Di and I missed. There had been some anti-British sentiment in the run-up to the handover and we thought there might be trouble on the streets on the night of the handover. So rather than venturing out to a grand black-tie party, we went to stay with our friends, Philip and Niki Goodstein, in Bangkok. Sarah was still living with us and, of course, she came too. Our reaction was completely overboard. There was no trouble and we missed a very good party. I greatly regret not being in Hong Kong for that momentous and historic occasion.

We watched the entire ceremony, held in the new wing of the Hong Kong Convention and Exhibition Centre, on television. It was pouring with rain all evening. The United Kingdom was represented by the Prince of Wales and Tony Blair, Prime Minister, and of course Chris Patten, Governor of Hong Kong. After various ceremonies and a cocktail reception for 4,000 guests, the official handover ceremony began at 11.30 on the night of 30th June with the Prince of Wales reading a farewell speech on behalf of the Queen.

Moments before midnight, the Union Flag and the last British colonial flag were lowered while the national anthem was played. A few seconds later, the flag of the People's Republic of China and the new Hong Kong regional flag were raised to the Chinese national anthem.

At 12.15 am on 1st July, Prince Charles and Chris Patten with his family bid the citizens of Hong Kong an emotional farewell at HMS *Tamar*, the Royal Navy's shore establishment on Hong Kong Island. They boarded HMY *Britannia* and sailed to the Philippines before heading back to the UK. They were escorted by HMS *Chatham*. The heavy rain never ceased.

It was a moving ceremony, which I remember vividly, and many tears were shed by the people of Hong Kong. Hong Kong was now an inalienable part of China.

Sadly, the Royal Yacht *Britannia*, launched in 1953, was decommissioned in December 1997 because the Labour Government, under Tony Blair, refused to fund the construction of a replacement vessel. Apparently, the Queen shed a tear or two at the decommissioning ceremony. *Britannia* is now permanently berthed in Leith, Edinburgh's port. Di and I visited the ship a few years ago – every detail was still in place.

Six weeks later, I was staying with Father in Lympstone in order to prepare Sarah for her first term at Wells Cathedral School. Having left Hong Kong in mid-July, Sarah was already in England and was staying with her mother.

On Sunday 31st August, I came down to breakfast to find my father looking very distraught. He told me that Princess Diana had died following a car crash in Paris early that morning. My father, who worshipped Diana, was visibly upset and I too was deeply shocked. Father had to take a service in church and I sat, dumbfounded, in front of the television, watching the news reports and later listening to a moving speech from Tony Blair.

I drove to Wells that day to meet Sarah on the Monday. I turned on BBC Radio. It was extraordinary: the only announcement was to say that the station would play 'mournful music' (or words to that effect) with no interruptions. I listened to one track, Pat Metheny's 'The Moon Song', which has haunted me ever since. At the time, I had no idea what was playing but I wrote to the BBC who subsequently provided the information.

The next day, Sarah and I queued at the school outfitters to buy her uniform and the many required, probably unnecessary, items before we returned to Lympstone. I cannot say that I was very experienced in such matters but nonetheless we had a successful shopping expedition. Sarah's first priority on reaching Lympstone was to have her school skirts shortened – despite strict rules concerning length – and one of Father's friends obliged.

Some days later, my father and I set off with a somewhat apprehensive Sarah to settle her into her new school. She was to join Haversham House, a girls' house under the charge of Mrs Smith. We said our goodbyes and she seemed happy enough to leave us. Father, Di (who had now arrived from Hong Kong) and I stayed the night in the Swan Hotel, one of our favourite hotels where we would stay on several occasions while Sarah was at Wells.

Princess Diana's funeral took place at 11.00 am on Saturday 6th September in Westminster Abbey. The British television audience peaked at thirty-two million, while an estimated 2.5 billion people watched the event worldwide.

We were due to check out of the Swan Hotel that morning but arranged with the hotel to keep our room until after lunch. The three of us watched the entire funeral in silence. It was a lovely late-summer morning and our room looked across the cathedral close to the beautiful west front, which made the occasion all the more poignant. It was a very moving service.

We heard nothing from Sarah for at least two weeks and grew increasingly concerned that she might be unhappy in her new environment. Finally, I telephoned Mrs Smith, her housemistress, to check that everything was all right.

'Mr Nourse, I'm sorry that you've not heard from Sarah,' Mrs Smith said, 'but you need have no concerns. She has settled in very well and has already made friends. She's just fine.'

'Oh, I'm so relieved to hear that. We were becoming quite worried that she was perhaps not very happy.'

'No need to worry. She is happy and in good hands.'

'Thank you, Mrs Smith. I'm so pleased we've spoken.'

We were a little miffed that Sarah had not been in touch but at least we were no longer anxious.

Sarah was happy at Wells and she did well. One of our more amusing memories were the letters from John Baxter, the headmaster, concerning her being caught smoking. He finally suggested we reduce her pocket money, which I think we probably did.

We visited her on several occasions, staying at the Swan Hotel.

She left in the summer of 1999, after a happy and successful two years, and went on to Southampton University.

Like her father and grandfather before her, she wanted to study medicine. Having obtained three B grades in her A levels, she was accepted on the course. However, at the end of year one, she failed her exams by a very small margin and simply couldn't face repeating the year. She really did not know what to do, having set her mind on medicine, so switched to psychology but her heart was not really in it. She also found it difficult to make friends on the course because they were all a year younger and new to university; it was not as enjoyable as it could have been.

At this stage, Sarah became anxious and began to think that she should be doing something different altogether. She was not entirely happy and was contemplating giving up the course but in the end – with some wise counsel from my father and a little persuasion from me and Di – she saw it through and graduated in 2003. Sarah tells me that she looks back without any regrets because medicine probably would not have been right for her. 'It was a blessing in disguise,' she says. Interestingly, I felt the same about medicine in later life.

It was at Southampton that she met Tom, now her husband.

Chesterton had been searching for a global partner for some time with a view to creating a strong international presence. There had been discussions with Jeff Binswanger of the Binswanger Group in the United States, which ultimately led to a strategic alliance known as Chesterton Blumenauer Binswanger or, more simply, CBB.

There had been a high-level conference in London, following which it was agreed that Chesterton Petty in Hong Kong would host a global CBB conference in 1997. I had not attended the London talks but, as director in charge of research, marketing and public relations, I was asked to take responsibility for organizing the Hong Kong

The view from Coastline Villa, Discovery Bay, 2008

My study in Coastline Villa, Discovery Bay, 2011

With Robert (left), Julie, Sandie and Michael after our Renewal of Vows ceremony in St John's Cathedral, Hong Kong, 11th November 2011

Lunch with friends in the Foreign Correspondents' Club, Hong Kong, November 2012

Before the St David's Ball, Hong Kong, June 2013

Attending the book launch of *Hong Kong High* at the China Clipper lounge,
The Peninsula Hong Kong, March 2014

At the Vidal Winery in Hawke's Bay, New Zealand, March 2014

With Jonathan (centre), Michael and Sandie in Coastline Villa, Discovery Bay,
October 2014

Me (centre) with members of the Foreign Correspondents' Club Wine Committee, February 2015

From left: Di, me, Kerstin, Sarah and Tom, Stockholm, July 2016

Sarah and Tom's marriage, Suffolk, 29th July 2016

Cooking with Jamie Oliver, London,
September 2016

With Margot after her christening, Suffolk,
28th May 2017

With Di and Margot, Suffolk, February 2018

At the Royal Academy of Arts, London, July 2018

Di with Krister on Wimbledon Common, August 2019

Our cruise ship, *Kraljica Jelena*, in Croatia, September 2019

With the bride and groom during the grand marriage celebrations in Madrid,
October 2019

At home in Barnes, October 2019

With Sarah at my 70th birthday dinner in the Oriental Club,
London, October 2019

With Christopher in the drawing room of No 10 The Cloisters, November 2019

Sarah, Margot and Pippa, September 2020

event, which involved delegates from all over the world and lasted two or three days. This was a huge task but we managed to identify top speakers and arrange meals in the best clubs and restaurants.

On the last evening, I took a party of about twenty out on our junk. The intention was to go to the pigeon restaurant on Lamma Island, where I had already ordered twenty-four pigeons. At the last minute, Jeff Binswanger asked if we could go to a restaurant which did not involve such a long journey, since many in the party had to be up very early the next day to catch flights home. So instead we took the junk to Sok Kwu Wan, also on Lamma Island but much closer, and enjoyed a very good seafood meal. The owner of the pigeon restaurant was not very happy with me!

The conference was a huge success and Jeff announced at the end that the next conference would take place in Wiesbaden, Germany, in 1999. There were two further global conferences: in Rio de Janeiro in 2000 and in Washington DC in 2001. I attended all these conferences, although it has to be said that my justification for doing so was moot since I was not part of the mainstream business.

The conferences were all fun – a mixture of work and play – but I have to say that the Rio trip was out of this world. Di joined this trip and we all stayed in a hotel on Copacabana Beach. Our friends from Binswanger had entered us all in the Rio Carnival. The atmosphere of the whole city was electrifying and the biggest carnival, held in the Sambadrome, was exhilarating, with bronzed samba dancers, pulsating music, energy, and applause from *cariocas* (locals) and visitors from around the world. When it came to dressing up for the parade in our fancy costumes, some of us decided to remain in the private box and watch. We avoided the rigmarole of donning our vividly coloured outfits and dazzling headdresses, and also waiting in the searing heat for the CBB march-past. We were very happy we made that decision: the participants in our team waited for two hours at least before they could even begin their parade.

Following the conference, Di and I flew to San Francisco, where we stayed for a few days before returning to Hong Kong. We had always wanted to visit this outlandish city, which exemplifies such an eclectic mix of architecture, people and culture. After all, it's where that magical Summer of Love, with all its glamour and ecstasy, began in 1967.

I believe many of us were quite sceptical about the alliance with Binswanger, which did not seem to fit with Chesterton's people and culture. The American approach to business, albeit refreshing in many respects, was very different from the more staid, professional style of the British. In 2005, Binswanger stepped back and announced that CBB would rebrand simply as Binswanger. The president of Binswanger explained: 'The fact that we highlighted different brand names in different parts of the world based on their historical value ultimately became more confusing than beneficial… it only makes sense to unify the brand under one name.' He was probably right: alliances with mixed branding can cause confusion. So Binswanger took a separate path while Chesterton Petty resumed business as usual.

I do not think that anyone at Chesterton was sorry about the demise of CBB and I am still not sure how we managed to get into bed with the Binswangers. I have often wondered if Binswanger were not simply using us as a platform to launch the Binswanger brand in Asia.

In 1998, I was toying with the idea of setting up a self-storage business in Hong Kong, where space was, and still is, at a premium. The vast majority of the population live in tiny high-rise flats with little room for storage. I was not aware of any such facility and therefore believed that it would be successful. However, I could not go it alone.

One of my younger colleagues in Chesterton Petty, Gary Beadell, often talked to me about moving out of the property field and working for himself. It struck me that he would make the perfect partner and I put the idea to him. He liked it and so we set up The Store House Ltd.

Our first facility was a floor in Cheung Fat Industrial Building in the western part of Hong Kong Island, which we fitted out with wooden storage units. The units let very quickly. Several other facilities followed, in different areas, where we upgraded the fit-out with steel units – minimal fire risk and much more secure.

The fitting-out involved substantial investment and I found that I was unable to raise the cash without selling investment property, which I was not willing to do. I therefore decided to reduce my shareholding from fifty to twenty per cent. Later on, Gary asked if I would sell my entire holding since he felt that I was not really committed and he was effectively running the business. I agreed and actually made a good return on my investment.

Gary was quite right. Although I came up with the original concept, I was not really interested in the day-to-day operations and was reluctant to invest as I preferred bricks and mortar. On the other hand, Gary was young, keen and very good at running and expanding the business.

He sold The Store House around 2015 for a significant sum. I felt a little aggrieved – with absolutely no justification. I should, of course, have retained a small shareholding – even five per cent.

A few years after setting up the self-storage business, I was invited to become a shareholder in a new business venture in Hong Kong: a franchise of an American organization, YoungBiz, which aimed to educate young people in financial literacy and foster proficiency in managing money.

The concept was excellent and relatively unknown in Hong Kong at the time. Four of us therefore agreed to invest US$50,000 each in the business. In the first year, the future looked promising and we succeeded in establishing links with local schools and attracting young students to participate in courses. However, it became increasingly clear that the business was undercapitalized and we were not able to secure the new funds necessary to invest in developing the business further.

At the same time, one of our shareholders was investigating the set-up in the United States, which raised some serious issues. YoungBiz was not all it appeared to be, apparently operating out of a tyre shop in rural Georgia. There were personal financial problems at the top – the irony speaks for itself – and there were threats of legal action following our decision to sever the relationship. In the end, we decided to close down the business. We had been misled and, of course, the legal threats dissipated very quickly. What could have been a highly successful business turned out to be an unfortunate investment. We were well out of it.

Since then, many programmes focusing on financial literacy for young people have been established, including the Youth Financial Education Programme set up by the Hong Kong Association of Banks in 2015.

I visited Angkor in Cambodia with Richard and another friend, Anthony Pettifer, who had made the arrangements, in 1998. Di was tied up with work and unable to join us. In those days, the number of visitors was manageable and we were able to move around quite easily. I believe the situation today is rather different, with swarms of people at every site.

One of the most important archaeological sites in Southeast Asia, listed as a UNESCO World Heritage site in 1992, Angkor extends to some 400 square kilometres and contains the remarkable remains of the different capitals of the Khmer Empire from the ninth to the fifteenth centuries. They include the famous Temple of Angkor Wat, built in the first half of the twelfth century and said to be the world's largest single religious monument, and, at Angkor

Thom, the Bayon Temple with its countless sculptural decorations. The architectural creations and bas-reliefs are extraordinary and quite unlike anything you would see in Europe.

We spent two days visiting the many sites in Angkor. I was astonished by the scale and detail of these monuments but I am not sure they compare with European architecture from a similar period, Chartres Cathedral in France being a fine example.

In the September 1998 issue of the Foreign Correspondents' Club magazine, I published an article, 'The riches of ancient Angkor', with many photographs of this extraordinary site.

In the late 1990s and for many years to follow, Di and I visited New Zealand, having made our first trip in 1996. We usually based our trips around one of the country's famous hikes – or tramps as the Kiwis call them.

Our first achievement, together with our friend Richard, was the Milford Track, a 54-kilometre walk in the Southland Region of the South Island. It is a spectacular walk which leads you across rope suspension bridges and extraordinary landscapes, past pristine lakes and raging waterfalls and over the MacKinnon Pass. The weather was not kind to us and we were sadly unable to enjoy the stunning scenery, although some would say that only when it rains – as it most certainly did for us – and torrents of water cascade down the steep mountainsides have you truly experienced the magic of the Milford Track.

We did not stay in the public huts en route but opted for a guided walk, which included four nights in private lodges. However, we still each had to carry a 40-litre backpack with all our personal belongings.

We spent four days on the track, although the first day involved little walking. Day three took us to the peak of the 1,154-metre-high Mackinnon Pass. The weather conditions were appalling, with driving rain, thick mist and sub-zero temperatures. Nearing what we thought was the top, we asked our guide how much further. 'Only another forty-five minutes to the peak,' he said. Our hearts sank and, when we finally arrived at the warm hut at the top, Di burst into tears – from sheer cold and exhaustion. Battling our way down, sometimes through waist-high water in swollen waterfalls, we arrived at Quintin Lodge for our third night. We revelled in hot showers and large whiskies were called for. After traversing the pass, our last day seemed relatively easy, although it was a long 21-kilometre walk.

There were about forty of us altogether, unlike our later walks on which there were fewer people and in some cases just us, two or three of our friends and the guide. The group was made up of Kiwis, some very posh Brits, a few Australians, a couple of Americans, a Swiss girl and two Japanese.

Dinner was served at tables of eight and we were given two bottles of wine per table. Our Swiss friend, Swissie, and the Japanese didn't drink so were much in demand as dinner companions! On the last evening, our table managed to bag Swissie. We were delighted, and then she announced, 'Tonight, I drink!'

They were a great group of people and we met some wonderful characters on the walk. We had enormous fun all the way. Di and I became very friendly with Trish, an interior designer from Auckland, and her husband, Ross. In fact, Trish and her sister, Liz, joined us for the Abel Tasman walk a year or two later. Ross declined! We have since stayed with Trish and Ross in Auckland a few times and in their holiday cottage in Northland.

The weather conditions were so bad on the day of our departure that our flight to Queenstown was cancelled. Rather than make the long journey by coach, we decided to charter a helicopter along with three Australians who needed to get home as soon as possible. One might think that flying a helicopter in these conditions would be more dangerous than a fixed-wing aircraft, but apparently not. The flight proved to be a terrifying experience. Flying through glacial valleys with black rock faces either side in near darkness, being buffeted by severe turbulence, is not to be recommended. Our pilot seemed to think nothing of it and was heard radioing ahead to order a Big Mac for his lunch. His nonchalance afforded us some comfort. And then we emerged from the storm into crystal-clear blue skies outside Queenstown; it was an extraordinary transformation.

The Milford Track was an adventure. Although we completed the Routeburn Track, the Abel Tasman Coast Track, the Nydia Track, the Tongariro Alpine Crossing (the name was changed to include 'Alpine' in 2007 to emphasize the potential exposure to extreme weather conditions) and the Coromandel Coastal Walk in the years that followed, none except perhaps the Tongariro Crossing could compete with the Milford Track in terms of spectacular scenery.

Often labelled as the 'world's finest single-day walk', the Tongariro Alpine Crossing is situated in the Tongariro National Park, a dual World Heritage Site acknowledged for both its natural and cultural significance. The 20-kilometre hike traverses active volcanic areas, including the peaks of Ngauruhoe, Tongariro and Ruapehu.

Having delayed the walk by one day because of poor weather, we were fortunate to have the most beautiful, clear day for our crossing. Parts of the walk were tough, including the Devil's Staircase, which climbs 200 metres from Soda Springs to South Crater. Descending from the Red Crater summit at 1,886 metres, we saw the stunning Blue Lake and Emerald Lakes, names that truly describe their colour. As a photographer, this was a remarkable walk, an opportunity not to be missed.

It is worth mentioning the Chateau Tongariro Hotel where we stayed. The hotel, situated in the heart of the national park and in the shadow of the volcanic peaks, was constructed in 1929 in the neo-Georgian style and offers an extraordinary sense of timeless elegance. We revisited this quirky hotel in March 2014 on our way from New Plymouth on the west coast of the North Island, where we were staying with my friend Frances McNulty from Touche Ross days, to Hawke's Bay on the east coast. We were going to stay with Penny Blundell and her partner, Sam Jackman (married to Lindy at the time of our marriage in 1991), who ran Millhills Lodge, a lovely property they had recently built just outside Havelock North.

We also made several visits to Australia during the 2000s. Our favourite place was Sydney; we loved the energy and sophistication of this cosmopolitan city. But I felt that Melbourne was a more mature city, more cultured and a little less brash. We also visited Adelaide, Brisbane and Perth, and the surrounding areas.

In 1998, Gordon Moffoot, who was now managing director of Chesterton Petty, suggested I should come back to the head office – now in CITIC Tower in Admiralty – and concentrate on marketing issues. I accepted and was given a generous office overlooking the harbour and could see the late-afternoon sun reflected in the office towers on the Kowloon waterfront, where I had been working a few days earlier.

I appointed a new marketing assistant, Michelle Chiu, who proved to be a great asset. She was proactive and had good ideas. She helped me enormously.

Gordon also wanted me to involve myself in the Residential Agency Department, where again there was potential for more business relating to tenancy management.

In 2001, a friend of Gordon, Philip Hamilton, introduced Chesterton Petty to Eric Tomlin, who owned and ran a property agency, Lynx Management, in Phuket, Thailand. I was dispatched to investigate and report back. I met Michael, Eric's partner, who gave me a tour of the island and explained how the business operated. One of the first properties he showed me was Baan Chai Nam, where Di and I would later buy an apartment.

We all got on very well and so began a business relationship that lasted for several years. It should be noted that Phuket at this time was very fashionable – the place to be – and there were numerous high-end developments under construction, looking for wealthy buyers.

We set up a joint venture, Chesterton Lynx, with an office on the east side of the island, not far from Phuket Boat Lagoon, with three or four staff. The business plan was simple: Eric and his team would identify suitable developments in Phuket and Chesterton Petty in Hong Kong would market them. I frequently visited Phuket to meet the developers and hopefully provide the international credibility of the Chesterton name, an essential component for marketing high-end property to sophisticated buyers in Hong Kong and elsewhere. We held exhibitions in Hong Kong and even at ExCel London, an international exhibition and convention centre in London's Docklands area.

Eric came to London with Khun Danang, one of our Phuket staff. Unfortunately, however, he refused to visit Hong Kong, where he was formerly a pilot with Cathay Pacific Airlines. The story goes that in 1993 Eric's French wife, Michelle, had a much-publicized affair with her dentist. Eric saw red and complained to the Dental Council, which quashed his plea to have his rival hauled up for misconduct. Eric therefore took his case to the High Court and, two years later, the Court of Appeal forced the council to conduct a full disciplinary hearing. Rather surprisingly, the real-life soap opera was brought to an end when the council absolved the dentist of professional misconduct. If I recall correctly, the reason why Eric would not come to Hong Kong was that his ex-wife would immediately claim fifty per cent of his assets. There may well have been tax issues too.

On 21st October 1999, I reached my half-century, a date that I remember thinking about often in my younger years. Of course, I had no idea what I would be doing at this time but I probably had concerns about reaching this grand old age. This landmark birthday called for a celebration and, well known for our parties, we arranged two celebrations: the first in London at the Oriental Club, followed by a second party at the Hong Kong Club.

Both parties were attended by seventy or eighty guests, who enjoyed drinks and canapés until well after 9.00 pm. Following the London party, all members of the family went to Rowley's Restaurant in Jermyn Street. My cousin, Frank Brumell, very kindly picked up the bill. We carried home an enormous suitcase full of presents. The following day, a group of us met for a long lunch in Brown's Wine Bar in Chelsea.

My former Swedish girlfriend, Kerstin, surprised me by telling me that she would come to the London party, after which I did not see her again until seventeen years later in 2016, when Di and I visited Finland and Sweden with Sarah and her fiancé, Tom. Kerstin invited us all out for a traditional Swedish dinner in Gamla Stan, Stockholm's Old Town. She insisted on paying. She had written to tell me she had had cancer and, during the evening, she assured me she was in remission. We waved an emotional goodbye as we parted. I watched her walk away. Three weeks later, on the night of Sarah's wedding, we learned that she had died. I was very upset. I had known Kerstin for nearly fifty years. I never met her husband, Dick, but we are now friends on Facebook.

In the summer of 2001, Di and I took my father to Rome. He had always wanted to visit Italy – as we had too – and had been trying to learn Italian for some time. A World Heritage site, Rome is best known for its architecture, ruins and art – and, of course, beautiful women and fine food. For us, St Peter's Basilica, the Forum and the Colosseum were probably the most memorable sites but the whole city is so full of rich architecture and art that it is difficult to know where to start.

One morning, my father felt unwell and stayed in the hotel to rest, but urged Di and me to go out and visit the Forum, as planned.

We returned at lunchtime to check on the patient, only to hear raucous laughter and jollity emanating from the hotel bar.

'Well, obviously the patient has fully recovered,' said Di.

'Yes, I am much better now. Nothing that a little whisky can't put right.' There he was, giggling away with an elegant blonde on each arm, chatting in his best Italian and clutching a huge glass of whisky. It would appear that it was not his first as he was having a high old time. 'Let me introduce you to my new friends, Francesca and Camilla.'

'I'm very pleased to meet you, ladies,' I said, marvelling at Father's aplomb.

We all had a drink together and then bade our farewell.

This anecdote sums up my father's *joie de vivre* rather well.

Our Rome trip was so successful that the three of us decided to visit Florence the following year and Venice in 2003. Venice has to be my favourite of the three cities. We stayed in a boutique hotel on the Grand Canal waterfront, overlooking the Church of San Zaccaria and a short walk from St Mark's Square. We spent our days simply wandering through the endless lanes and taking in the magical Renaissance and Gothic architecture of this beautiful and unforgettable city.

Our last visit to Italy was in 2004, when we decided to take Father to visit Claire Hiscock, an old friend of Di from university days. She lived with her husband and two daughters, Lara and Elena, in the Le Marche region on the Adriatic coast. Claire and the children had also visited us in Rome and Florence. We flew to Bologna, where we stayed for a couple of nights before making the four-hour train journey to Macerata.

My father, now aged eighty-two, was beginning to have some heart problems and was walking with a stick. He was a little fragile, so the train journey we were about to embark upon caused some anxiety. Bologna railway station was packed with people and, having finally located the correct platform, a last-minute switch in platform was announced. We struggled with luggage and stairs – poor Father was suffering, but we made it onto the train.

I must at this point report an amusing incident, although it was certainly not funny at the time. During the second half of the journey, the train came to a halt. The line was blocked with hundreds of people. We could hear cries of '*Il Papa, il Papa.*' Apparently, there had been some sort of convocation with the Pope nearby and the assembled pilgrims had decided to storm our train because their special transport had been cancelled or delayed. Hundreds of young people crowded onto the train and, quite simply, overran our First Class compartment. When the time came to get off the train, we literally had to fight our way through a wall of humanity. It was a nightmare.

My father decided that we should return to Venice, a city that he now loved, in 2005. In his words: 'This will be my last visit to Italy.' He agreed to book the flights. Sadly, we had to cancel the trip as his health was declining and he was not up to travelling overseas. We are still due a return visit to Venice.

At 8.45 pm on 11th September 2001, Di and I were having a quiet drink in the Hong Kong Club. On the television screen in the corner, we watched an extraordinary series of events unfold. It was a clear Tuesday morning in New York when an American Airlines Boeing 767, loaded with 20,000 gallons of jet fuel, crashed into the north tower of the World Trade Center. The impact left a gaping, burning hole near the eightieth floor of the 110-storey skyscraper, instantly killing hundreds of people and trapping hundreds more on higher floors. This devastating event became known as 9/11.

Initially, nobody in the bar was quite sure what we were seeing. Was this a film or was it an event on the news? Once the volume on the television was turned up, it became clear that this was genuine breaking news.

Eighteen minutes after the first plane hit, a second Boeing 767 appeared out of the sky, turned sharply towards the World Trade Center and sliced into the south tower near the sixtieth floor.

We were all in a state of disbelief and shock as we listened to the live reports from New York. Di and I went home and, like many others, spent much of that fateful night watching the remarkable scenes of horror and destruction on television. There were two other plane attacks shortly afterwards: one hitting the Pentagon in Washington DC, the other crashing before its intended target was ever known.

The hijackers were Islamic terrorists financed by the al-Qaeda terrorist organization of Osama bin Laden. The total death toll was almost 3,000. This was the beginning of a new era: the 'War on Terror'.

At about this time, I applied for a place on the Cambridge University Certificate in English Language Teaching course run by the British Council in Hong Kong. It was highly competitive as there were only about a dozen students on the course. My reason for wanting the qualification was as a back-up career in uncertain times and also a line of work to pursue in semi-retirement. My situation was unusual. I had no teaching background and it was difficult for me to suggest that I was planning to go into a teaching career on a serious basis. There were a number of discussions and, perhaps surprisingly, I was accepted for the course.

The course ran on a part-time basis over several months. We had an interesting group of students, the teaching was exceptional and the course content of the highest quality. We were put through our paces: apart from lectures and practicals, we were required to teach actual students, having prepared full lesson plans and assembled appropriate teaching materials. This was in the days before hi-tech teaching wizardry and I spent a good deal of time creating pictures from raw materials and using felt-tip pens on whiteboards to demonstrate a point. I enjoyed the whole course enormously; it was challenging and gave me a whole new perspective on life.

My business plan was simple: to approach companies and offer English-language programmes for about a dozen middle- or senior-management employees, the courses to be run in their boardrooms. I would have virtually no overheads. I had little interest in teaching on a one-to-one basis.

In the event, I continued to work with Chesterton Petty and my plan never came to fruition. However, I was approached by a company called Live English, which operated in very much the same way (as well as teaching children, an area in which I did not become involved). We undertook a number of courses in business English, often with a focus on customer relations, and also one-off sessions. It all worked very well until the owner began to think that lessons should be conducted in Cantonese, which he felt would make it easier for the students – even if they would never hear an English accent. In my view, his approach was totally wrong but clearly the services of native-English teachers in his company were on the way out.

Through Live English, I also taught the diploma courses in written and spoken business English for the Hong Kong Management Association for one year. The classes were made up of about twenty-five students, working for a wide variety of organizations, and took place from 7.00 pm to 9.30 pm once a week in Kowloon. This was a real challenge, handling students of different abilities and from all sorts of backgrounds, but it was enormously rewarding.

Back in Phuket, one of our first instructions, in 2002, was to market The Plantation, a new development of apartments in Kamala on the west coast of Phuket. The development was situated in Rimhat Road, affectionately known as Millionaires' Row, reflecting the price level of Allan Zeman's famous Andara Resort & Villas next door and other developments in the area.

On 12th October 2002, thirteen months after 9/11, two bombs ripped through the Kuta tourist area of Bali, leaving 202 people dead. Among those killed at Paddy's Irish Bar and the nearby Sari Club were people from twenty-one countries, including eighty-eight Australians, thirty-eight Indonesians and twenty-eight Britons. Eleven members of the Hong Kong Football Club attending a rugby tournament also died.

The terrorists, an Islamist group, claimed that the bombing was part of a jihad, or holy war, to 'defend the people of Afghanistan from America'. Ironically, more Australians and Indonesians lost their lives than Americans.

Not only did the bombings have a devastating effect on tourism in Bali, with the number of visitors tumbling, but also the property market in Phuket was adversely affected. Prospective buyers pulled out and we lost at least two buyers in The Plantation.

In November 2002, we bought our first home in Hong Kong: a top-floor flat in The Honourgarten, a three-storey block in Consort Rise, an older area of Pokfulam. We owned investment properties in SoHo but this was the first purchase of a real home, in which we would live, in Hong Kong. It was a small flat, with two bedrooms and one bathroom, but it had a huge roof terrace on which we entertained frequently.

There was an illegal structure on the roof – a covered area – which the Government Buildings Department later identified on one of its many predatory building surveys. We came home one day from a holiday to find a notice demanding that it be removed. We were somewhat shocked but knew we had to comply. The roof terrace was never quite the same but we bought a vast cantilevered umbrella which proved to be an adequate substitute.

A few months later, the SARS (severe acute respiratory syndrome) virus reached Hong Kong. From 11th March up to 6th June 2003, a total of 1,750 cases were identified and, during the same period, 286 people died of the disease in Hong Kong. Before the advent of SARS in Hong Kong, neighbouring Guangdong Province in mainland China had experienced an intense outbreak of this atypical pneumonia, which was later called SARS. From March onwards, SARS was detected in other countries in Asia-Pacific and globally. Over 8,000 people from twenty-nine countries and territories were infected and at least 774 died worldwide. The virus was relatively short-lived and died out eight months after it was first detected in China. The World Health Organization declared SARS to be contained on 5th July 2003.

As I write these words in London in December 2020, the world is experiencing one of the most serious coronavirus pandemics ever: COVID-19. The number of cases and deaths is huge when compared with SARS. The spread of this contagious disease has been frightening and nobody quite knows how it will pan out, although a number of vaccines are being rolled out in the UK in the coming months. Interestingly, Hong Kong appears to have contained the situation well – perhaps because the government and people have learned from the SARS experience seventeen years earlier.

In the summer of 2004, Di and I bought a top third-floor apartment in Baan Chai Nam, situated at the southern end of Bang Tao Beach on the west coast of Phuket. I had first seen this estate on my exploratory trip to Phuket in 2001. Unlike so many residential developments in Phuket, Baan Chai Nam was a mature property, built amongst lush tropical gardens running down to the sandy beach.

We often walked along Bang Tao Beach, some six kilometres long, observing groups of fishermen at work in their traditional long-tail boats before watching the sun go down with a glass of chilled white wine. We would then frequently dine in one of the many restaurants in Surin village, a short walk away.

The apartment was a very attractive two-bedroom property with a pitched roof and exposed timbers, an open-plan living area and a balcony. The development comprised only twenty-three units, mainly houses and duplexes, and benefited from a lovely beachside swimming pool, tiled in a deep-blue colour, where we used to enjoy many an afternoon.

We spent a great deal of time making our new apartment into a second home, although we had always planned to let it on a short-term basis to cover the costs, and held a house-warming party later in the summer. Our first letting was over the Christmas period, which of course commanded a very good rent.

Unusually for us, we decided to spend Christmas 2004 in Phuket and, since we had let out our apartment, made a booking in the Marina Phuket Resort, one of my favourite hotels where I often stayed on business trips, at the very southern end of Karon Beach. We had a detached villa, built partly on stilts over the sea, with views across the bay. We booked Christmas Day lunch in the Green Man pub in Rawai, a ten-minute taxi drive, where the owners had set up a long communal table for those guests who were not in a party. Despite some misgivings, we had a fun lunch with good food and met some interesting people. After a long day, we went back to our room early and watched television. We decided to walk along the beach the next morning.

On Boxing Day morning, we did not feel our best and decided to sit by the pool in the morning and go for our walk after lunch. At approximately 10.00 am, a tsunami struck the west coast of Phuket, flooding and causing severe damage to almost all beaches, including Bang Tao, Patong, Karon, Kamala and Kata. There was no warning. No one had any idea what was happening. Phuket and the west coast of Thailand were approximately 500 kilometres east of the earthquake epicentre and the tsunami took just two hours to reach its shores.

While we were sitting by the pool, Di decided to go back to our room to fetch some water. She returned in a state of shock, having witnessed a massive wave retreating from the shore, carrying with it cars, sections of buildings and, for all we knew, people too. We rushed back to the room and I saw for myself the devastation. Although our room was partly supported on stilts sitting over the rocks and water, there was no damage whatsoever to the room. I have always found this extraordinary; it was as if the tidal wave had simply bypassed our room in favour of the beach and waterfront.

We locked our room and hurried back to the main hotel. On our way, we glanced at the steps leading to the beach and saw there were numerous Thais running in all directions – the Thais are not known for running. We made our way to an elevated grassy area in the grounds of the hotel where everybody seemed to be assembling. Nobody really knew what had happened; many were in a state of shock and crying. The word 'tsunami' was unknown to most people in those days.

Leaving Di with other guests on the hill, I made my way down to the waterfront with my camera. Di asked me not to go but, as a photographer, I was determined to record the situation. The amount of damage was unbelievable – shattered buildings, upturned cars and trucks, torn-up roads and flooded areas. There were not many people about; I suppose they had retreated inland. It looked like a war zone.

I returned to the hotel and Di and I both went back to look at the devastation. As we wandered around in disbelief, a police motorcyclist drove through, shouting, 'Get to higher ground, get to higher ground, the big one is coming.'

We panicked. I knew the area well and led us to a hill nearby where we found many, many people gathered. I was still in my swimming trunks and shirt, with camera; Di was more fully dressed and had her handbag. We had left our towels, books, sun creams and the like by the swimming pool.

We waited and we waited. We were frightened. We didn't talk very much, but I knew we were both thinking that we might die here. I was looking at trees onto which we could hold but, of course, such thoughts were futile. If a second tsunami hit, we would all be obliterated by the massive force of the water. The hill was not high enough and there was nowhere else to go.

As time passed, the fear subsided a little – no second wave so far. We noticed a small hut nearby and went to see if we could find food and drink. There was nothing except crates of Carlsberg. The beers were not cold but we didn't care. We came to a deal with the caretaker and negotiated a supply of beers to keep us going for however long.

At one point, some people who had parked on the hill decided to set off and escape inland. We asked a man with a truck if we could jump in the back, to which we received a curt 'no'. I am not sure why I asked because I knew that the only road was on the coast and would be blocked; they would not have got very far with the devastation all around.

Later, someone came and said we could all walk down to a house halfway down the hill and see the news on television. We decided to stay as high up as we could. Eventually, after many hours of waiting on the hill and rather hungry, we realized we had to go somewhere. It seemed there would be no second wave. Di would not return to our hotel room that night so we walked to a nearby hotel on the hill, the Peach Hill Resort, which I knew.

The hotel lobby was heaving with people escaping from the waterfront, some whose accommodation and possessions had been destroyed – who had nothing left. We were very lucky to get a room. We collapsed with shock and emotional exhaustion. Our phones were pinging with numerous text messages asking if we were OK. We were. We lived through that fateful day, which will remain etched on our minds for the rest of our days.

The following day, we returned to our own hotel and gathered up our belongings, which we had abandoned by the swimming pool, and packed our luggage. We were due to return to Hong Kong, so we checked out and made our way to the airport. Much to our surprise, flights appeared to be operating fairly normally. However, the check-in desks were packed with people trying to get out of Phuket. Fortunately, we had a confirmed booking and were able to leave without any problems.

Despite being one of the most badly hit coastlines, only about 250 people were killed in Phuket, including around 100 foreigners. Many more were injured and many were missing. Khao Lak, a smaller resort eighty kilometres north of Phuket, was hit much worse, with some 4,000 deaths. The death toll in Thailand was nearly 5,400, of which 2,000 were foreign tourists. Very sadly, many bodies were never recovered.

The earthquake, with a magnitude of 9.1-9.3, was the third-largest ever recorded, killing some 230,000 people in fourteen countries, making it one of the deadliest natural disasters in recorded history.

Like every other beach on the west coast of Phuket, Bang Tao Beach, on which our apartment was situated, was severely affected, with a wave of up to four metres driving its way through our beachside development, largely destroying two single-storey houses right on the beach and causing untold damage to the ground-floor units behind. Since our apartment was on the third floor, we suffered no actual property damage but of course the electric power failed and the entire infrastructure was torn apart. Our first tenant had to evacuate.

The damage took several years to repair and the property was not fit for letting during this period. We visited but, with the swimming pool out of commission and major rebuilding taking place, it was not much fun.

Once the property was restored and up and running, we found that long lets were far easier to obtain than short lets – perhaps because the position of our apartment, with no sea view, made it less suited to short-term holiday breaks. I stayed there several times while on my business trips and, at some stage, we entered into longer-term lettings, meaning that we could not enjoy the flat very often.

In the end, we reluctantly decided to sell the property. There were some changes in property-title laws being introduced by the government, I was no longer working in Phuket and Di did not feel very comfortable staying there with memories of the tsunami still vivid in her mind. It took over two years to find a buyer, who turned out to be a friend of one of our neighbours in the development, and we very sadly said goodbye to our much-loved holiday home in 2014, ten years after having bought it. On reflection, I suppose that it was really the tsunami that took away the gloss.

After several years of losses and changes in ownership, our parent company, Chesterton International in London, went into receivership in 2005. The commercial operation of the company was sold to Atisreal (now part of BNP Paribas) while the residential division was bought by the Consensus Business Group and two joint-venture partners. The Chesterton Petty directors attempted to buy out the Chesterton Petty shareholding held by Consensus without success.

As a result, the major working Hong Kong shareholders were now searching for a suitable merger partner with sufficient clout to buy out not only the UK interest but also the non-working and minor shareholders in Hong Kong. However, discussions with a number of suitors came to naught as the holdings of the non-working shareholders were too great, meaning that a very substantial investment would have been required.

There was a small group of shareholders who were pushing to make changes – oust the old guard and bring in new shareholders, perhaps with a view to 'filling their boots' if and when a partner willing to pay a good price could be found. I believe there may have been all sorts of shenanigans surrounding the whole affair.

One afternoon, Gordon Moffoot, the managing director, and I were attending a meeting with a prospective client, a developer of a residential complex and golf course in Spain. Following the meeting,

Gordon told me that he had been asked to resign as part of the management buy-out. I think by this time he had had enough of the ongoing trials and tribulations. He was ready to retire and agreed to resign on condition that he could maintain a consultancy role for six months.

One of our directors, who was at the forefront of what appeared to be a coup, immediately took over as managing director. He did not last long and jumped ship to a competitor. I believe the move had already been planned. The then finance director took over as managing director – again for a short period.

Later that same afternoon, one of my co-directors – also in the vanguard of change – visited my office and asked me to resign too. I don't think the new managing director had the temerity to face me. My days as an executive director of Chesterton Petty were numbered – not in the least unexpectedly and with some relief.

George Doran, who joined the original firm, Tony Petty & Associates, shortly after it was set up in 1972 and served as managing director and chairman of Chesterton Petty, sold his shares at the same time.

Clearly, there was a new broom…

The Chesterton Lynx joint venture was still operating, and it was agreed that I could remain in the Chesterton Petty office and continue to run the business and market Phuket property. Although I was no longer an executive director of Chesterton Petty (with a very posh harbour-front office), I was still part of the business, interacting with my colleagues on a daily basis. This arrangement certainly eased my change in status.

At about the same time, a merger agreement was reached between Chesterton Petty and the Hong Kong office of Knight Frank, the famous British real-estate consultancy. I was obviously not involved in the discussions.

Part of the deal with Knight Frank apparently required that there could be no further reference to 'Chesterton', although in fact the word did continue to appear in various forms. The long and the short of the Knight Frank agreement was that Chesterton Lynx could no longer exist in its present form.

Perhaps with some prescience, I personally had already set up a company called Homes International, and it was this company, owned 100 per cent by me, that continued to work with Lynx in Phuket following the Knight Frank merger. We had, of course, lost the Chesterton brand, which would make our marketing efforts more difficult; nonetheless, we operated for some time with a degree of success.

Phuket was rapidly growing in popularity, with more direct flights to the island and an increasing stock of high-quality property. As a result, some of the big real-estate names were setting up there and beginning to dominate the market. The Lynx and Homes International partnership could not really compete, particularly when it came to international marketing, and I decided to call it a day in 2007. I closed down Homes International and that was the end of our Phuket business. Sadly, my partner, Eric Tomlin, with whom I had worked since 2001, died in 2010.

Chapter 11
The Next Chapter

2005-2017

Following my departure from Chesterton Petty in August 2005, I met Kasyan Bartlett for a drink in the Foreign Correspondents' Club. Kasyan and I first met in the early 1990s and have remained friends ever since. He owned fifty per cent of Pacific Century Publishers Ltd, a publishing company best known for *Over Hong Kong*, a unique and spectacular aerial portrait of Hong Kong's astonishing geographical and cultural diversity with extended captions, published annually and recording the rapid transformation of the territory from year to year. Kasyan's partner, Keith Macgregor, who subsequently left the business, is another good friend who now lives not far from us in Barnes. He is a famous Hong Kong photographer and has a remarkable collection of Hong Kong photographs dating back to the 1970s.

In those early days before computers, Kasyan and I used to meet for lunches and discuss whether computers or interactive television would lead the technology revolution (we did not have computers in the office until about 1992). We also talked often about switching roles:

my moving into the world of publishing and photography, a long-held dream; and Kasyan, somewhat disillusioned with publishing, becoming a wealthy property magnate. The switch never took place, of course.

Kasyan first approached me when I was a director of Chesterton Petty and suggested we should publish our own company calendar, which we did. And then in 1997, Chesterton Petty's twenty-fifth anniversary, we agreed to publish a special anniversary book with Kasyan's assistance: we underwrote Keith's book, *An Eye on Hong Kong*, with a customized Chesterton dust jacket and an eight-page corporate insert bound into the book. Keith was enormously grateful and has published many updated versions of the book as well as other photography books since. He wrote in the front of my personalized copy of the book:

To Philip

Thank you very much for trusting me in this book even before you had seen a single photograph! I am very chuffed that you and your company are my first corporate client.

When Kasyan and I met all those years later, in August 2005, a partial role switch did actually take place.

'I'm sorry to hear about Chesterton Petty. What happened?' Kasyan asked.

'It's a long and rather unsavoury story.' I explained the background.

'Well, I have a thought. Would you be interested in helping me run the business?'

'You mean like we used to discuss over twenty years ago?'

'Yes, exactly. You see, I want to spend more time in the UK and I need someone to manage the business on a day-to-day basis. I'll be back and forth, of course, but I need someone I can trust to hold the fort while I'm away.'

'I think that sounds fantastic, but do you think I'm up to it? I don't know much about running a publishing business.'

'You'll learn very quickly and I can give you guidance. You know, once you get into it, you'll see how it all works. But in any event, as a first task, I would like you to review the staff and give me your thoughts on their abilities and potential.'

'It all sounds great, Kasyan. I really appreciate your giving me this opportunity at a time of big change for me.'

Of course, I jumped at Kasyan's offer – a lifesaver, a new chapter in my life in a field in which I had always wanted to be involved. We discussed how it would all work and then reconfigured the office in Hillwood Road, which had a superb view over Tsimshatsui and West Kowloon, to accommodate an extra desk in Kasyan's office. And so began a new partnership.

I was not working with Kasyan on a full-time basis; in fact, I was wearing several hats. At this stage, I was still running the Phuket business out of Chesterton Petty's office, usually in the mornings, before crossing the harbour to Hillwood Road in the afternoon.

I had also set up my own business, Infocus Media, in June 2003, providing editorial, design and photography services for a variety of clients, including companies in the property, retail and interior-design fields. The marriage with Pacific Century Publishers was perfect and much of the consultancy work I undertook for specific Pacific Century projects and publications was channelled through Infocus Media.

Let me give you a little background on Infocus Media. Although I have always been an active photographer and set up a website, Imagenasia (www.imagenasia.com), to showcase and market my Hong Kong and Asia-Pacific images, it was not until 2001 that I received my first real break in commercial photography.

The managing director of The Banyan Tree, a shop with several branches specializing in Asian-themed furniture and accessories, commissioned me to photograph the store's entire product line for a new brochure. This was a formidable task and took several weeks to complete since I could not work on the project full-time (I was still a director of Chesterton Petty). However, working with Jo Allott, the product manager and buyer, we completed the job on time and published a high-end glossy brochure.

At this stage, I had not converted to digital photography and, in order to produce the highest-quality images, I bought a Mamiya RZ67, a professional medium-format camera. I also bought a professional Polaroid camera for test shots before using expensive medium-format transparency film. I loved my Mamiya and subsequently bought a Mamiya 6, a medium-format rangefinder camera, for travel photography. I converted to digital in 2003 and now use Canon, Fujifilm and Sony cameras.

The Banyan Tree commission led to other work, notably with Gail Arlidge Design, for whom I photographed numerous residential interiors. Gail was one of my major clients, and we had fun setting up and dressing rooms before I photographed them. On one occasion, I photographed the interior of a motor yacht owned by her daughter and son-in-law. I am sad to report that Gail died unexpectedly in July 2018, bringing to an end a very good working relationship that lasted for more than ten years.

All sorts of other interesting jobs followed, including working with property firms, shipping and storage companies, finance companies and Jason Wordie, a well-known Hong Kong author and historian.

In 2006, my daughter, Sarah, introduced me to VisualMedia, a London-based media company for whom she was working. I undertook a number of assignments for this company, including photographing Barclays Bank's advertising hoardings at Hong Kong International Airport for their advertising and PR people and taking staff portraits for Holiday Inn Hotels.

However, the most interesting assignment was an aerial shoot of a drilling rig off the east coast of Kalimantan, the Indonesian section of the island of Borneo, for Salamander Energy. The ancient Bell helicopter in which I flew rattled a good deal and I had some serious concerns for my safety but I lived to tell the tale. This assignment also involved a day photographing the people and equipment on the rig and taking a boat to meet some very elderly residents of a nearby village.

Flying to Balikpapan, I managed to drop my mobile phone down the loo – lost forever, or so I thought. On receiving my next rather large bill, I found numerous phone calls had been made from Indonesia. The mind boggles.

In January 2009, I approached the Hong Kong Club, of which I am a member, with a view to upgrading its rather old-fashioned monthly magazine. Working with Sarah, who was by then a graphic designer and living back in Hong Kong, I submitted a detailed proposal and won the job.

We produced the entire magazine, *The Club News*. This was a stressful job with strict deadlines and, in 2015, the design of the magazine was taken up by another company and I focused on the editorial component. To this day, I continue to work on the magazine with the club, now my most important client. I have also photographed almost every part of the interior of the club.

Sarah and Tom wanted to return home and left Hong Kong in 2009. Tom didn't want to work with the London office of his employer and instead transferred to Monaco, where they lived for a year before returning to England. However, Sarah and I continued to work together on *The Club News* and other projects for a number of clients.

During this period, my father was becoming increasingly unwell. He had begun to experience the first symptoms of heart failure in April 2005. I made my usual solo spring visit to Lympstone in May, when he and I tried to finalize his own memoirs, which I published posthumously in 2007, and we had already cancelled the planned second trip to Venice.

After four months in and out of hospital, including a two-week stay in the Royal Brompton Hospital in Chelsea, where heart-valve replacement and bypass operations were considered but ruled out on account of his age (eighty-two) and general frailty, he came home to live out his remaining time. A succession of live-in carers, a stairlift and his circle of close friends eased his increasingly uncomfortable months; but for a man so self-sufficient and mentally alert, his gradual decline and dependence on others was deeply distressing to him.

Di and I both returned to Lympstone in September and were joined by Christopher and Sarah. Father was remarkably chipper, despite his declining health. The four of us had fun and Christopher came up with a plan for all of us to have Christmas at home in Lympstone.

I vividly recall sitting on my father's bed while he was having his afternoon rest and promising him that I would come back to see him at Chinese New Year at the end of January as well as the planned Christmas trip.

'Beany,' he said, 'I honestly don't think I will be here then.' (Beany and Flapper were affectionate names by which my father often called me, the latter apparently derived from my early attempts at pronouncing Philip.) I left his bedroom because tears were beginning to well up in my eyes and I did not want Father to see me so upset.

The Christmas plan did not come to fruition. My father telephoned me in Hong Kong after we had left Lympstone and said that he could not cope with the prospect of a houseful, so Christopher booked a nearby house where he, Charles, Di and I could stay. As it happened, my father went into Exmouth Hospital on 19th December and the Christmas house party was cancelled.

Di and I flew to London shortly before Christmas. Christopher had agreed to meet us and come down to Devon for a night or two. However, on arrival at Heathrow at 5.30 in the morning, he told us that he could not now drive us since his detached retina, for which he had already had an operation, had caused more problems and he would have to go back to the hospital straightaway. He was unable to warn us before we left Hong Kong as the problem had only flared up overnight. Not wishing to go into central London in order to catch a train to Devon, we found that we could take a National coach from Heathrow to Exeter, from which we took a taxi to my father's house.

Di and I visited Father in hospital several times. It was a 'cottage' hospital with around eight beds in his ward. The care seemed excellent and I spoke to the doctor on duty on more than one occasion. Father slept much of the time but was in surprisingly good spirits when he was awake. On Christmas Day, a nurse brought around a bottle of bubbly before lunch.

'Cheers, Beans, and happy Christmas.'

'Happy Christmas,' we said, raising our glasses, tears in our eyes.

The nurse did her circuit and Father demanded a refill. He was in good form and we laughed together.

We did not visit him on Boxing Day but returned on 27th December, a day or two before we were due to fly back to Hong Kong. I found it very difficult to say goodbye at the end of our visit. We promised, once again, to come back and see him at the end of January and Di asked if it would be even colder by then. I said no – even the bluebells would be coming up.

Father replied in typical fashion, 'No, too early for bluebells; snowdrops at the end of January.' Those were really his last words to us. It was an emotional parting and I left with a heavy heart, knowing that I would not see him again.

My father died in Exmouth Hospital on Tuesday 3rd January 2006. Christopher phoned me early on 4th January (Hong Kong is eight hours ahead of Greenwich Mean Time). I was deeply upset and very sad, although the phone call was not unexpected. I had already said my farewell; it was just a matter of time. I was very close to my father, with whom I had a special relationship, and knew that I would miss him enormously.

A Thanksgiving and Requiem Eucharist, with much music and following a rubric devised largely by him, was held in Lympstone Parish Church on Friday 27th January in the presence of some 300 friends and family.

After the funeral service, the bells pealed in celebration of his life and the whole congregation, choir and clergy repaired to the village hall for refreshments. It was a splendid party, a typical 'village do', with plenty of food and drink and much laughter. It was just as my father would have wanted.

The following Monday, quietly and without music or ceremony, he was cremated at the Devon and Exeter Crematorium; and early the next morning – a cold, grey day, the dew still wet on the grass – his ashes were placed beside those of my mother in Lympstone churchyard, a few feet from the graves of his maternal great-grandparents and in the shadow of the church where my grandparents were married in 1909.

Following Father's death, Christopher and I received a small inheritance (my father was a priest!), which enabled me to buy a one-bedroom flat in Mosque Street in SoHo, Hong Kong, which we had renovated by a designer friend. We had already bought investment properties in Hong Kong but this was undoubtedly our favourite. It overlooked the nineteenth-century Jamia Mosque with an open view across SoHo and Mid-Levels. Di and I stayed there sometimes, between lettings. I rather regret selling this flat some years later; not only because it was a charming flat, but also because it served as a kind of shrine to my father.

*

The timing of my father's death was unfortunate as far as my work was concerned, but Kasyan understood entirely and we quickly caught up. I was immediately involved in reviewing the company's operations and staff. Pacific Century Publishers was a small company employing five or six staff besides Kasyan and me. We did not make any immediate changes but the contents of my report provided useful information for staff assessment and planning for the future. As part of our strategy, we decided, in 2010, to rebrand the company: partly because we were sometimes assumed to be a subsidiary of a much larger company with a similar name but primarily because we felt the need to adopt a more modern name. After much brainstorming, we settled on Bonham Media Ltd. (My own company, Infocus Media, began life as Infocus Communications. I changed the name shortly after we created Bonham Media.)

One of the first publications in which I was involved was *Cementing The Link*, a book we produced for Gammon Construction about the Hong Kong–Shenzhen Western Corridor, opened for traffic on 1st July 2007 and now known as the Shenzhen Bay Bridge. The book was published in 2007.

Like so many of the book projects we undertook, the subject matter was stimulating and deeply interesting, involving huge amounts of research for both the text and the images. Shortly after we completed *Cementing The Link*, we embarked upon the production of *Over Hong Kong – Volume 8*. This involved many hours of aerial photography with Kasyan in the Heliservices helicopter – frequently with me on board – selecting the best and most suitable images and writing extensive descriptions. The *Over Hong Kong* series always sold well, especially to visitors to Hong Kong.

We published a number of books concerned with the history of Hong Kong, including *From Sedan Chair to Jumbo Jet: An Illustrated History of Transport in Hong Kong* and *The Amazing Adventures of Betsy & Niki*, a fascinating history of the two aircraft that were the founding fleet of Cathay Pacific Airways. We published many other books too, usually Hong Kong-focused, as well as producing corporate brochures for various companies, including property companies with whom I had close contacts.

In 2013, we published a new edition of *Hong Kong Picture Perfect*, a portfolio of original photography, which included a large number of my own photographs. The last book we published before closing the company later in the year was *Macao: People and Places, Past and Present,* a massive 500-page journey through the enclave of Macao, written by Jason Wordie, with whom I still work today.

During the 2010s, the publishing business became increasingly difficult, with audiobooks, digital books, Kindle and other media seriously competing with the printed book. In our case, we also had a limited market in the sense that sales were largely dominated by local residents and visitors to Hong Kong, a small market when compared with the United Kingdom or the USA. Our print runs rarely exceeded 5,000 copies, whereas a normal print run in a larger market might easily be 20,000.

Kasyan asked me on a number of occasions if I would be interested in buying the business. I think he wanted to move on to pastures new. Of course, I could see the writing on the wall and, in any event, I did not feel that I could successfully grow the business without the help of a seasoned publishing professional. I declined his offers and, in retrospect, I am very glad I did. I would undoubtedly have lost money.

However, Ronna Lau, a colleague with whom I worked very closely, did enter into an arrangement with Kasyan and took over the business, enabling Kasyan to free himself completely from the company. Ronna was fortunate because her father, Moby, owned office premises and we were therefore able to operate without the burden of rent. He also ran a production company and was able to provide support.

Sadly, business declined. The demand for corporate books weakened; not only because more and more companies were turning to the Internet for marketing and promotion but also because corporate budgets seemed to become tighter every year. In October 2013, Ronna reluctantly took the decision to close down Bonham Media. It was a sad day and the end of a very happy eight-year association for me.

Shortly after we had announced the decision, Kasyan's father, Magnus, approached me and asked if I would like to work on a consultancy basis with his company, Odyssey Publications. The company is best known for its travel guides but I was involved in other projects, including the launch of *Hong Kong High: An Illustrated History of Aviation in Hong Kong*, a book celebrating more than a century of aviation in Hong Kong – from 1911 to 2014. The launch was hosted by Sir Michael Kadoorie in the China Clipper, an aviation-themed suite on the highest level of The Peninsula, immediately below the hotel's rooftop helipad.

Again, business was difficult and it became apparent that the company could not afford my consultancy fees, albeit they were very modest. I was also beginning to make plans to return to the UK and it made sense for me to wind down my activities in mid-2015, although I retained a desk and a computer until Magnus advised me he was closing the office to work from home at the end of September.

Our last ten years living full-time in Hong Kong were spent in Discovery Bay, a self-contained enclave on Lantau Island with a population of some 20,000 and no private cars – only buses to the ferry pier, a few local taxis and hugely expensive private golf buggies for those who can afford them.

Discovery Bay has a certain magic. A friend who visited us shortly after we moved made the comment that 'Discovery Bay is the Monaco of Hong Kong'. In a sense, he was right. There is a riviera feel about it, with cafés and bars lining the waterfront, a beautiful beach, numerous boats, parks, lush gardens and a stunning backdrop of mountains. There are luxury houses overlooking the bay as well as high-rise apartments, and the residents by and large feel they belong to this special place.

In search of a downside, I could suggest there are far too many children – hence the moniker 'Delivery Bay' – because it is a very child-friendly environment. For the same reason, dogs abound too but they are generally better behaved!

We sold our flat in Pokfulam in 2007 to a special buyer whose offer we could not refuse. It transpired that the buyer was trying to buy all three flats in the block, which she ultimately succeeded in doing, so that she could convert them into one house. Had we known, we could probably have extracted a slightly higher price but we were happy.

And so began a new life in Discovery Bay, somewhere I had first looked at in 1986. We bought a three-bedroom apartment, which we totally renovated, on the first floor of Coastline Villa, a terrace of six-storey blocks overlooking Discovery Bay Marina. The apartment faced south-west and was very light, with the late-afternoon sun casting an orange glow on the many yachts and live-aboard boats moored in the marina and, in the near distance, Hei Ling Chau and Sunshine Island. The marina was a community in itself and a hive of activity, with residents pottering about the jetties and sailors rigging their yachts before heading out to sea. It was magical and, at night, the lights of the vessels glimmered on the water to the gentle sound of shrouds chiming in the night breeze.

During our nearly ten years in Coastline Villa, we enjoyed entertaining and hosted splendid lunches and dinners for eight or so friends at our walnut dining table. We also spent most Christmases in Coastline Villa, preparing the full works for a formal sit-down meal for eight or ten. Many people came to stay, both family and friends from around the world. In the autumn, when temperatures were bearable, we would sit by the pool of the Discovery Bay Marina Club, of which we were members, sipping a beer or two.

It was a beautiful flat. Of the seven homes we lived in over thirty years in Hong Kong, Coastline Villa was the home we loved most.

We continued to travel in Asia-Pacific, wanting to see as many interesting places as we could before our likely return to the UK.

We made a memorable trip to Luang Prabang, the former royal capital of Laos. Unfortunately, our visit coincided with the Lao New Year or *Songkran* celebrations, which seem to consist mainly of a 'festival of water', during which both locals and visitors take great delight in throwing water over passers-by from buckets, water pistols or any other suitable vessel. Foreigners were certainly fair game and we spent a good deal of time attempting to avoid water attacks. It was all good, harmless fun but it did rather curtail our sightseeing and photography.

We also visited Phnom Penh, the bustling capital of Cambodia. It was once known as the 'Pearl of Asia' and considered one of the loveliest French-built cities in Indochina. Besides the architecture and temples, our main interest was in visiting the 'Killing Fields' and the S-21 prison camp, where people perceived by Pol Pot and the Khmer Rouge as educated, lazy or political enemies were detained and tortured. The prison camp is now the Tuol Sleng Genocide Museum, where Khmer Rouge torture devices and photographs of their victims are displayed. Little did these frightened people know that they would be marched to the 'Killing Fields' to be brutally murdered and buried in shallow pits. Looking at these photographs, the tiny cells in which the prisoners were kept and the burial grounds was an extremely moving experience.

I made another visit to Beijing – my last as it happens. Di was on a business trip, and I decided to go on a photographic mission to expand my limited collection of China images. The first day was fine and clear; I was able to capture some great images. On the second day, I returned to the new Summer Palace, which I had not visited since 1993. Unlike my first visit, when visitors were few and far between, the tour groups were overwhelming; it was a nightmare. The pollution made it worse; it was almost impossible to photograph the palace from across the lake. Di and I were to join up on day three and go out together. On waking up, however, we could not even see across the street for thick smog. We cut our losses and caught a flight home immediately. I am sorry to say that this is the polluted Beijing of today.

I celebrated my sixtieth birthday in October 2009 in our usual style – drinks and canapés in special surroundings. As with my fiftieth, we hosted two parties. On this occasion, we held the London party at the Royal Automobile Club in Pall Mall; the second party was held at the Hong Kong Club.

Not unlike my fiftieth birthday, when Kerstin flew in from Stockholm to join my party, I had another surprise: Vicki Lang, a friend from Windsor days, whom I had not seen since we had lunch together when she was passing through Hong Kong in the 1990s, accepted my invitation and announced that she would be flying in from Switzerland for the occasion. It was an extraordinary experience meeting up with an old friend thirty-seven years on. We now keep in touch regularly.

In November 2011, Di and I decided to celebrate our twentieth wedding anniversary in a special way and renew our marriage vows. We had planned to have this ceremony on our twenty-fifth anniversary, but we were not sure whether we would still be in Hong Kong and wanted John Chynchen, who married us in 1991, to perform the ceremony in St John's Cathedral.

It was a simple, heart-warming ceremony attended by a few

close friends. I chose the reading, from 1 Corinthians 13, 1-13, words that I remember so well from St George's Chapel days, and I gave Di an emerald ring which I had specially made by a jeweller in Hong Kong we had known for years. We asked John to arrange two professional singers, Raymond Fu and Shirley Yeung, who sang at our request John Rutter's 'The Lord Bless You and Keep You'. They performed this piece beautifully; we were both moved to tears.

Following the ceremony, we walked down Garden Road to the Hong Kong Club where we hosted a large party in the Garden Lounge, a stunning fourth-floor venue with floor-to-ceiling windows overlooking the colonial-style Court of Final Appeal Building and Chater Garden. It was a fun party with all our good friends and Michael Dalton, whom I first met in 1989 and who sadly died in August 2018, gave a lovely speech.

Di and I had booked into the JW Marriott in Admiralty, a short walk from the club, where we spent a very comfortable night. The following morning, quite by chance, we bumped into Michelle Ching, a friend from Singapore who had also been at the party and, unknown to us, was staying at the same hotel. And so the party continued: Bloody Marys on the hotel poolside terrace followed by a long lunch in the Foreign Correspondents' Club.

A year later, on 8th November 2012, my dearest friend, Robert, married Josie, whom he had known for eighteen years, in Hong Kong. He employed her as his live-in helper in 1994 and, after four years working for him (and for us on a part-time basis for two years), she returned to the Philippines. Although Robert had returned to the UK in the early 2000s, he and Josie remained very close, frequently speaking on the phone and Robert regularly visiting Manila.

As best man, I made many of the arrangements with Di's help, including a wedding dinner in the Foreign Correspondents' Club for twelve close friends at which I gave a speech. It was a very happy day.

The following May, Robert telephoned us to tell us that he had been diagnosed with liver cancer. We were devastated. By September, it was clear that he did not have long to live and, on Tuesday 15th October, Di and I flew to London and went straight to his home in Winchester.

We arrived in the evening and were greeted by Josie. Robert was in bed, very weak, but was able to welcome us. He knew we had come, that we were there.

'Can I offer you a glass of wine?' he said in his inimitable way.

'That would be wonderful,' we replied and Josie was sent off to open a bottle.

'I have a small gift for you, Di.'

It was a vintage copy of her favourite classic, long out of print, *Sinister Street* by Compton Mackenzie. Sadly, he was unable to inscribe it. Di held his hand and those were the last words he was able to speak to us.

On the Wednesday, Robert's condition declined and he was taken to hospital. We stayed with him much of Thursday and Friday, during which family and friends visited. I remember Robert's father, who was then ninety-seven, distraught, looking over his dying son and saying, 'Goodbye, my friend.' And he was a friend. Robert's nephew, Nick, arrived from Paris late on Friday afternoon.

At 11.30 pm on Friday 18th October 2013, Robert Ernest Atkinson died in the Royal Hampshire County Hospital in Winchester. He was sixty-three and had been married less than a year.

We went to the hospital to say a sad goodbye to our closest friend and, the next day, we had to return to London before flying back to Hong Kong. We were in a very sombre mood but a lunch, already arranged with Christopher, Charles, Sarah and Tom, helped to lift our spirits.

Robert's funeral took place on 30th October at St Peter's Church in Winchester. Having spent time with him during his final days, we felt that we could not return to England again for the funeral. However, Hugh Purser gave a beautiful eulogy and included some of the words I had written:

> *We've thought so often about how lucky we were to have Robert as a friend. And for days now, we have been asking ourselves: how could such abundant generosity, such kindness and such joy in living – how could all these things just disappear? The answer is, they don't. Because every one of us who was privileged to call Robert a true friend will do everything possible to ensure that Robert's high standards, his concern for others and his good humour are remembered always.*

On 7th November, the eve of his first wedding anniversary, we organized a small wake for Robert in the Foreign Correspondents' Club.

'Farewell, my friend. You are sadly missed.'

I should make brief mention here of the 2014 Occupy Central movement or Umbrella Revolution, the first serious, violent protests in Hong Kong since the 1967 riots.

Demonstrators were demanding the right to nominate and directly elect the chief executive along with other demands. The protests followed a declaration by the Standing Committee of China's legislature, the National People's Congress, on 31st August 2014 that any candidate for the post must be vetted by an electoral committee, which would undoubtedly be made up of tycoons, oligarchs and pro-Beijing loyalists.

It was an extraordinary time. The occupation began during the last few days of September, with police quickly using tear gas in an unsuccessful attempt to clear the protesters. Many roads were blockaded by tens of thousands of protesters who set up camp and prevented the movement of traffic. I remember walking down Chater Road in the heart of Central District, usually humming with traffic – and yet not a single car in sight. Turning left and walking past the Hong Kong Club and into Connaught Road Central, I could see a carpet of tents and umbrellas stretching all the way to Admiralty, the demonstrators weaving their way through their new makeshift homes.

The protests did not affect us significantly but there was, of course, inconvenience from time to time in the sense that we might have to make a long detour to reach our destination – or we simply could not get there at all.

The protests and resulting violence spiralled in the days and weeks that followed, and it was not until the end of November that bailiffs and police started to move in to clear an occupation site in Mongkok. The Admiralty and Causeway Bay sites were cleared by mid-December.

The pro-democracy movement has not subsided and 2019 saw some of the worst protests and violence ever experienced in Hong Kong.

Having decided that we would make our permanent home in the UK, with a plan to move in 2017, we were casting about for a suitable pied-à-terre in Discovery Bay; a second home which would enable us to maintain our links with Hong Kong and also escape the British winter.

After visiting many properties, we found a small flat on the eighth floor of Onda Court, an attractive curvilinear block overlooking the bay and Tai Pak Beach, with the mountains of North Lantau forming a grand backdrop to a riviera setting. We renovated the flat and moved in on 18th March 2016, having sent a shipment of furniture and possessions from Coastline Villa back to the UK. We had a housewarming party on 22nd April.

Sadly, we had to lose our Filipina live-in helper, Mary, who had worked for us for seventeen years, having joined us in early 1999 when we lived in Realty Gardens. In the early years, she did not live with us but stayed in a shared flat – or a boarding house, as the Filipinas call it. She started to live in when we moved to Discovery Bay, where we had proper maid's quarters. Happily, Mary was able to find another job in Discovery Bay, which she has also come to love.

Mary was very loyal to us and we decided to pay for her daughter's final two years at Cebu Doctors' University in Cebu, where she was training as a nurse and now practises.

We still own our flat in Onda Court and spend three or four months in residence over the winter months, usually celebrating Christmas in Hong Kong and returning to London in the spring.

On 31st May 2016, Di finally retired from PricewaterhouseCoopers after some thirty years, albeit with a break of about five years in the early 2000s when she was working for a former PwC partner. A leaving party was held a few days before in the office in Edinburgh Tower in the Landmark. Di's bosses, Tony Kwan and Tracey Pugh, gave her two embossed prints from designer Megumi Takami's 'Farewell My Hong Kong' series, which are based on Japanese artist Kiyoko Yamaguchi's watercolour drawings. She was also presented with a caricature of her everyday self by the office amah's husband, who created photofits for the police.

Three weeks later, we were back in London on an extended trip, having stopped over in Singapore to see our friend Julie. We then headed off to Finland and Sweden (courtesy of Finnair, who had lost our luggage for four days on a previous trip to Hong Kong). We met Sarah in Helsinki, and Tom joined us a week later in Stockholm after Di, Sarah and I had taken the night boat to Sweden. Sarah was five months pregnant.

At this stage, Tom was a director of Njord Offshore Ltd, operators of crew-transfer vessels for offshore wind farms, while

Sarah was working part-time for a design and branding company, Holy Cow! We were still working together on a few projects.

On 29th July 2016, Sarah and Tom were married in St Peter's Church, Stutton, near their home in Holbrook, Suffolk. Tom had insisted that the men wear morning coat and, despite my initial reluctance, I must say that it made the day all the more special.

Since I was giving Sarah away, Di made her own way to a pew on the left-hand side of the church, one or two pews behind Elaine and her husband, Michael, and other members of her family. Elaine turned to Di and said, 'Di, you're Sarah's other mother. You must come and sit here in the front with us, please.' Di was very touched that Elaine felt she had played such an important part in Sarah's life.

I proudly walked my daughter down the aisle before a simple ceremony attended by family and friends. After the service, the statutory photographs were taken before we all returned to the house in Holbrook where we enjoyed a wedding lunch.

I, of course, made the first speech. However, the small informal family setting, with only about a dozen guests, meant that I could get away without making the traditional, rather lengthy father-of-the-bride's speech. Nonetheless, I spoke for some minutes, with both gravitas and humour, and quoting Churchill's words: 'My most brilliant achievement was my ability to be able to persuade my wife to marry me.' In the case of Sarah and Tom, who had known each other since university days, I am not sure who asked whom – I suspect there was not too much asking.

It was a lovely day: warm and sunny and filled with joy and bonhomie. I could not have wished for more.

Their first child, Margot Olivia Mehew, was born on 9th November 2016. We were back in Hong Kong and heard the news the following day. We visited Sarah, Tom and Margot in Suffolk in mid-December – our first experience of a grandchild. Of course, Margot was only six weeks old, wriggling and beginning to discover her fingers and feet as well as giving us the occasional smile.

Having just returned to see Margot, we decided to spend Christmas in England and were invited by Christopher and Charles to join them with friends in their home in Earl's Court. We stayed with our friends, Gerry and Sheona, in Edinburgh over the New Year and returned to Hong Kong at the end of January.

We made a trip to New Zealand in February 2017. We stayed with Sam and Penny in Millhills Lodge in Hawke's Bay for several weeks before driving north to the Coromandel Peninsula, where we completed the Coromandel Coastal Walk. We then headed back to Auckland and spent a few days with Ross and Trish McKay, whom we first met on the Milford Track walk almost twenty years before.

We officially left Hong Kong on 26th April 2017. After thirty-three very good years, we both felt a pang of remorse; and yet this was not a sad parting. We had our second home in Onda Court and knew that we would be returning later in the year and for many years to come.

Chapter 12

Coming Home

2017-2020

On 27th April 2017, British Airways flight BA28 touched down at Heathrow Airport at 5.35 on a cold but sunny morning. Spring was in the air.

Di and I were coming home to England. Of course, we had been home at least once a year to see family and friends but this was a decision to make our permanent home in England and become officially resident – certainly as far as the taxman was concerned. It was not our plan to forsake Hong Kong, which we love, and we return every year to escape the English winter, more often than not spending Christmas there.

On our return, we stayed in our pied-à-terre in St Paul's Court in West Kensington, having also spent three months there in the summer of 2016 in order to see how we felt about living back in England. St Paul's Court is a development of houses and flats, built in mellow red brick in the 1980s and set around an attractive well-landscaped garden. We bought our two-bedroom duplex in November 2011 as a bolthole, knowing that it would be far too small as a permanent home, especially with family visiting.

We have many friends in St Paul's Court, which is a real community. One of our regular get-togethers was the wine-appreciation group. We usually met monthly, tasting far too many wines and staggering home across the lawn. We also enjoyed summer parties with residents. Even though we have now moved, we still attend the wine meetings and are often invited to parties and other events.

And so, perhaps a little reluctantly, we started searching for a larger home, looking at properties in Oxford, Winchester, Windsor and elsewhere outside London, as well as numerous properties in West Kensington, Richmond and Barnes. Over a two-year period, we must have viewed thirty or more properties, finally settling on Richmond or Barnes as our preferred locations, but still not having found a suitable home.

After spending Christmas in Hong Kong, we arrived back in London at the end of January 2018, without much will to start the search again. However, quite by chance, we came across a penthouse flat in Barnes Waterside – considerably over budget – and immediately loved it. We exchanged contracts at the end of April before heading back the following day for a planned trip to Hong Kong and Bali. We had finally found our forever home. The purchase was completed on 27th June.

Barnes Waterside is an upmarket development in north Barnes, built by Berkeley Homes in the late 1990s on a site that was previously derelict land and disused reservoirs owned by Thames Water. Berkeley Homes, who entered into a partnership with Thames Water and the Wildfowl & Wetlands Trust, purchased ten hectares of the site for the development and funded the adjoining London Wetland Centre, opened in 2000.

The master planners, JTP Architects, were briefed to design a village community made up of terraces and crescents with a variety of large villas, town houses and flats in period style. The whole development is set in beautiful gardens, with a 'village pond', adjoining the River Thames on the eastern perimeter and the Wetland Centre to the south. The famous Harrods Village, formerly a soap works, candle-making factory and sugar refinery and later Harrods' Depository, is sandwiched between Barnes Waterside and the river on the north-eastern boundary. It was converted by Berkeley Homes into 230 apartments and thirty-eight town houses, all designed to maintain the style of the original buildings. The entire Barnes Waterside and Harrods Village complex is, in my view, a design masterpiece.

Our penthouse flat comprises an elegant drawing room, a unique octagonal dining room, an eat-in kitchen, a study, three bedrooms, three bathrooms and a cloakroom. We also have a large garage and an additional outside parking space.

The flat is unusually light and enjoys a panoramic view from Putney Bridge in the south-east to the towers of Hammersmith Bridge in the north. We can see the London Wetland Centre and beyond to Richmond Park, Wimbledon and Putney Commons and the Surrey Hills on the horizon. We often see a flight of geese, almost within touching distance, sweeping past, wings beating, heading home to the wetlands as the sunset casts a coppery glow across the western sky.

Besides redecorating the entire flat, we decided to replace the kitchen, which turned out to be a complete nightmare with a succession of delays, deliveries of the wrong or damaged equipment, and even deliveries to the wrong address. The saga began on day one when the new kitchen was due to be delivered early in the morning, which would enable the contractors to make an immediate start on the installation after ripping out the existing kitchen, completed by late morning. The apparent delivery failure made the contractors, appointed by the suppliers, suspicious – and so was I. A little later on the same day, the suppliers telephoned to tell me that they could not deliver for three weeks. And so it went on – for some ten weeks

– until the kitchen was finally completed, two months behind schedule. It was extremely fortunate that we were able to delay our move-in date but we never told the suppliers, giving us a great deal more ammunition to support our later claim. The only high points of this lamentable experience were that we finally ended up with a high-quality kitchen, we were able to negotiate a one-third reduction in the cost and we inherited some excellent contractors who still undertake jobs for us today.

We finally moved in on 3rd August on a very hot day. We had been advised that the lift would be out of order and had explained this to Sam, the boss of our removal company. He thought nothing of carrying the entire contents of our St Paul's Court home up four floors and his team did so with aplomb.

We love Barnes. It is very much in the manner of a leafy country village, much of which is now designated as a conservation area, and boasts individually owned outlets, including a butcher, fishmonger, cheese shop and bookshop, as well as cafés, restaurants and the luxury Olympic Studios cinema, once a recording studio made famous in the 1960s by The Rolling Stones and many other well-known artistes.

The centre of the village is dominated by Barnes Pond and opposite is the famous Sun Inn, one of nine very good pubs in Barnes that we know. Round the corner is the Saturday Farmers' Market, selling all kinds of fresh and home-made foodstuffs.

We often walk along the towpath, the ribbon-like River Thames meandering majestically past the Royal Botanic Gardens in Kew before reaching Hammersmith Bridge and heading south past Barnes and east to Shivering Sands Towers in the North Sea.

When the tide is low, waders can be seen probing the mudflats for worms; and during the full and new moons, the river is swollen by spring tides that can sometimes flood the towpath. The cycle of the tides is constant and yet the character of the river is forever changing.

*

There were several reasons for coming home to England: not only to be closer to family and friends, but also to appreciate the changing seasons, which I missed enormously in Hong Kong, and have the opportunity to explore unknown parts of Britain and Europe.

It is true that Hong Kong's subtropical climate has four seasons, but they cannot compare with the joy of the changing seasons in Britain: spring flowers coming into bloom, the madness of summer, the colours of cascading autumn leaves and the bleakness of winter, perhaps with a dusting of snow.

Having not had the chance to explore much of Europe while we were in Hong Kong, we were looking forward to having it on our doorstep and, so far, have visited Portugal, France and Spain.

In Portugal, we visited the ancient city of Porto in the north-west of the country, with its labyrinth of narrow cobbled streets and immense architectural patrimony. We also made a short boat trip down the Douro River. The river valley is best known for its port vineyards, the hilly riverbanks dominated by large signs bearing the names of famous port producers such as Cockburn's, Sandeman and Taylor's. The town of Pinhão marks the start of port production and boasts a charming railway station with hand-painted tiles (*azulejos*) depicting the grape harvest.

Lisbon, the vibrant capital, has more of a metropolitan feel than Porto and is, of course, a much larger city, also endowed with fine architecture, majestic avenues and a deep-rooted heritage. However, for me, Porto has the edge – as Lisbon's quieter sibling with its old-world charm and hidden magic. After Lisbon, we stayed with our dear Brazilian friends from Hong Kong, Joel and Odila, who retired to Estoril, a seaside resort half an hour's drive west of Lisbon on the 'Portuguese Riviera'.

A year later, following a trip to Paris with Christopher and Charles and their good friends, Krister and Kevin, we took the train to Montpellier. We made a special visit to the Picasso exhibition at the Musée Fabre before staying with more Hong Kong friends, Mick and Linda, in their charming house in Saint-Pons-de-Mauchiens in what used to be called the Languedoc-Roussillon region (now part of Occitanie). The name of the village is derived from *mauvais chiens* (meaning 'wicked dogs'), who supposedly devoured a feudal lord from the castle.

Saint-Pons-de-Mauchiens is a medieval *circulade* village, built in concentric circles around the twelfth-century castle, perched on a hill with a 360-degree panoramic view of vineyards, mountains and, on a clear day, the Pyrenees. Our friends' house is just a few minutes' walk from the Church of Sainte-Marie and Saint-Pons which adjoins the ruins of the castle.

We then travelled on to Barcelona, perhaps best known for Gaudí's Sagrada Familia, a 'cathedral of the twentieth century'. The work completed during Gaudí's lifetime was declared a World Heritage Site in 2005. The planned completion date is 2026, the year of the centenary of Gaudí's death. Construction will have lasted 144 years. The cathedral is indeed a remarkable sight and a moving experience, simply because of its neo-Gothic and modernist architecture, massive size and the extraordinary variety of themes and colours. I would like to return one day – perhaps in 2026.

In addition to exploring Europe, we have also enjoyed seeing more of Britain and have made tours of the West Country, Scotland and Wales, catching up with many friends along the way.

At this point, I must report on our narrowboat cruise on the Oxford Canal, which I was rashly persuaded to join. Di had often spoken amusingly of her canal trips in the 1970s when she and a group of close friends, including Gillie and her sister Annie, Jenny, Tony and Peter, had great fun exploring some of the UK's canals.

It seemed that Di, Jenny and Gillie, egged on by her husband, Gavin, were determined to relive the experience. Not long after, we were signed up for four nights on an eight-berth narrowboat.

I must admit that I couldn't work up too much enthusiasm about the planned trip; not because I don't like boats and water, but because I find narrowboats and canals rather dull, and the living quarters very cramped. Of course, had it been a luxury boat on the Canal du Midi in southern France, preferably with Rick Stein on board as resident chef, my perspective would have been entirely different. Nonetheless – and despite the rather gloomy September weather – I thoroughly enjoyed myself.

We still love travelling around Asia, of course, and when we returned to Hong Kong for Christmas 2018, Di and I decided to go to Penang, a small island off the west coast of Malaysia. We spent a delightful week relaxing in the sun and seeing friends from Hong Kong before flying down to Singapore to stay with Julie.

Di and I first visited Penang at Easter in 1987. We have always had a soft spot for this former British colony. The capital, George Town, is fascinating, the ancient centre having been inscribed as a UNESCO World Heritage Site in 2008. We returned in later years, staying in hotels on Batu Ferringhi beach and, on one visit, I spent two days photographing butterflies for greeting cards which I subsequently published. I visited again in May 2012 and made a rather tedious and uncomfortable four-hour train journey from Butterworth to Kuala Lumpur, where Di was running a conference at the Hilton hotel.

In September 2019, we went with Gerry and Sheona on our first-ever cruise, which Di had reluctantly agreed to, despite her fear of the sea. We spent seven nights aboard the *Kraljica Jelena*, an elegant 50-metre motor yacht with nineteen cabins, cruising the Dalmatian islands off the west coast of Croatia. We flew to the ancient city of Split, where we spent two nights before setting sail for the island of Brač, our first overnight port of call. Thereafter, we visited Hvar, Mljet, Dubrovnik, Korčula and Makarska, mooring for one night in each port before returning to Split, where we disembarked.

All the places we visited had their own particular magic and charm, and we had a marvellous time exploring historic towns and enjoying breathtaking views. Our mornings were more often than not spent luxuriating in the sunshine on the top deck and swimming in the crystal-clear sea before feasting on a three-course lunch and cruising to the next overnight haven. We came to know our fellow passengers, all of whom were English-speaking, and enjoyed their company enormously. It was a memorable experience which we would happily repeat.

We followed the cruise by returning to the beautiful island of Hvar for three nights with Gerry and Sheona. Hvar Town, with its attractive harbour and buildings, is sadly becoming a favoured destination for the rich and famous; apparently, every night is party night aboard the luxury yachts that line the waterfront during the summer months. Nonetheless, Hvar is a magical place: steeped in history, beautiful architecture and a sun-drenched landscape carpeted with lavender fields lining the turquoise sea.

The following month, we made a glorious trip to Madrid to attend the marriage ceremony of Elaine Doran, youngest daughter of George and Donna Doran, and her fiancé, Ravi. George was chairman of Chesterton Petty when I joined the company in December 1988 and we remained good friends until his death in June 2020. The lavish marriage celebrations lasted three days, with champagne all the way.

We spent four nights in Seville before taking the train to Madrid. Seville, the steamy-hot capital of Andalucia, captivated me. Its historic centre, dominated by a colossal Gothic cathedral and the Giralda bell tower, which I climbed, is an intoxicating mix of resplendent Mudejar palaces, baroque churches, plazas filled with fragrant orange trees and winding medieval lanes. A photographer's dream, I loved it.

In Madrid, we were preoccupied with celebrations and champagne. Comparisons are unfair, but somehow I felt it lacked the history and charm of Seville. We enjoyed the parks and gardens, for which the city is well known, and spent time in the Parque del Buen Retiro photographing the Monumento a Alfonso XII, opened in 1922, and the Palacio de Cristal, a glass conservatory with a cast-iron framework, built in 1887, comparable to the architecture of London's Crystal Palace and the Palm House at the Royal Botanic Gardens in Kew.

Having visited the Picasso exhibition in Montpellier, the 'Picasso 1932' exhibition at the Tate Modern in London and the Musée National Picasso-Paris, we wanted to visit the Museo Nacional Centro de Arte Reina Sofía, which houses Picasso's *Guernica*, which in 1981 was sent to Spain from New York in accordance with Picasso's directive that the painting be moved there only after democracy had returned to the country. *Guernica* is a massive oil painting, completed in 1937, regarded by many art critics as one of the most moving and powerful anti-war paintings in history. Di and I were truly mesmerized and stood in silence for many minutes looking at this extraordinary work of art.

Retirement has also provided an opportunity to renew my interest in various activities. I decided to take up chess again, not having played since school days. I found a chess master during our 2019 sojourn in Hong Kong and embarked upon a series of one-to-one lessons. I have found enormous satisfaction in the intellectual challenge of the game and continue to play but, like many of my 'sporting' ventures, I do not seem to make any real progress. The same story applies to my snooker, a game that I have played for many years but rarely win, and golf.

Di has taken up riding again. She rode horses for a living at Tadworth stables in Surrey in the early 1970s, looking after and exercising livery horses, giving riding lessons and riding her own horse, London Melody, a lively thoroughbred, at shows and dressage events. She has always loved horses – and horse racing too in Hong Kong. She has often spoken of riding again and had a couple of rides in Hong Kong, but they were not very satisfactory because the horses at Beas River Country Club, where we stayed, were retired racehorses and extremely temperamental. She had not ridden for many years. It was Krister, Christopher and Charles's friend and a competent horseman, who persuaded Di to ride with him when we were living back in London. After a couple of sessions on the mechanical horse at Wimbledon Village Stables (I also had a brief session and was apparently very good), she started riding on the common. (I have never much liked horses, despite the origin of my name – from the Greek *philos hippos*, meaning lover of horses.)

Talking of horses, Sarah and Tom kindly took us to the Newmarket races. As tradition dictates, we prepared a superb picnic, with bubbly, smoked salmon and all the usual accoutrements. We sat on folding chairs at the rear of the car to provide some protection against the elements: it was eight degrees Celsius and raining – in early May.

If the weather conditions were not enough to bring us to our senses, we were then rather bemused by the hordes of uncouth young people roaming the enclosure, girls skimpily clad in their 'designer' outfits, many of them inebriated and running for the loos.

Di said to one of the girls in the loo, 'You must be frozen in that outfit.'

'Don't worry, luv, I've got me thermals on under this lot.'

I always had an idea that going to the races in England would be the 'real' thing: down to earth, wellington boots, standing next to the racetrack. I think I'll stick with the more sophisticated version in Hong Kong.

Two thousand and nineteen was a difficult year for both the United Kingdom and Hong Kong. One is reminded of 1992, a year fraught with disasters for the Queen, which she described in a speech as an *annus horribilis.*

The UK was struggling with political infighting and a parliamentary deadlock following uncertainty and indecision over the process of withdrawal from the European Union after fifty-two per cent of the population voted to leave in June 2016.

After the Conservative landslide victory in the general election on 12th December 2019, the withdrawal agreement was ratified and the UK finally left the European Union at 11.00 pm on 31st January 2020, beginning a transition period during which the UK and EU negotiated their future relationship. On Christmas Eve 2020, the UK and European Union finally agreed a treaty that meant the UK would restore national sovereignty, taking back control of its laws, borders, money, trade and fisheries. After the deal was concluded, Prime Minister Boris Johnson said: 'It changes the basis of our relationship with our European neighbours from EU law to free trade and friendly cooperation.'

In Hong Kong, a very different story was unfolding. In June 2019, protests began against a proposed extradition bill, which would have allowed criminal suspects to be extradited to mainland China in certain circumstances. Critics and anti-government politicians feared the proposed legislation could undermine judicial independence, would give China greater influence over Hong Kong and could threaten the freedoms enjoyed by the people of Hong Kong. Huge numbers of people took to the streets and the controversial bill was finally withdrawn in September, but the protesters claimed it was 'too little, too late'. The protests continued throughout the year and how the situation will evolve in the longer term remains to be seen.

On 30th June 2020, the Chinese government introduced a national security law in Hong Kong, which appears to have quelled the protests and rioting. However, the legislation is highly controversial. Only time will tell how the law is implemented and whether the principle of 'One Country, Two Systems' survives.

*

Family and friends are at the forefront of our life in London. Sarah and Tom live with their two daughters in an old house, a former butchery, in Suffolk, six miles south of Ipswich, sandwiched between the River Orwell and the River Stour. Margot is now four years old and attending nursery school. Philippa (usually known as Pippa) Rose was born at 4.25 am on 28th July 2020.

Despite the relentless duties of motherhood, Sarah appears calm and relaxed. They both enjoy the 'country life', Tom is a keen sailor and they love growing vegetables in the kitchen garden – generally leading as green a life as they can. They have recently acquired a beach hut on the banks of the River Stour, which has become a focus of family life and where they spend a good deal of time.

And we have so many friends, scattered throughout the country and overseas, with whom we have kept in touch while living in Hong Kong. When we meet up with friends in the UK now, it feels as if we have never been away.

I celebrated threescore years and ten on 21st October 2019. Unlike previous gatherings, involving around eighty guests, Di felt that we should make this birthday party a more intimate affair, so we only invited my closest family members and a few friends. Twenty-four of us congregated in the Ante-Room of the famous Oriental Club in London for champagne before sitting down in the elegant, wood-panelled Library for a gourmet three-course dinner accompanied by fine wines. My son-in-law, Tom, and a close friend from Hong Kong, Anthony, made speeches, to which I replied. It was a very special evening, which I shall always treasure.

Two weeks later, Christopher, who was sadly unable to join my birthday dinner, arranged a visit to Windsor Castle through Charlotte Manley, Chapter Clerk of St George's Chapel – a belated birthday present, perhaps. This visit far exceeded our expectations, Charlotte giving us an extensive tour of No 10 and No 24 The Cloisters, the two houses in which we lived from 1957 to 1967.

It was an extraordinary experience. More than fifty years on, here I was revisiting the rooms where we grew up and lived for ten formative years – many virtually unchanged, others transformed in one way or another to become part of St George's House, opened in 1966. Memories flooded my mind. It was an emotional journey, followed by sung evensong, with a full choir, in the chapel.

There was a sense of coming full circle.

Looking back over my threescore years and ten, my life has been full of excitement and happiness, but also some disappointments and sorrow. I know that I am deeply emotional, sometimes wistful in the autumn of my life, and easily moved by my perceptions, especially choral music – perhaps because of my years in St George's Chapel.

When I see the world today, with war, poverty, disease and social unrest, I know that I have been truly privileged to enjoy life to the fullest and to share my innermost self with my wife, Diane.

And I am lucky to have reached threescore years and ten.

> The days of our years are threescore years and ten;
> and if by reason of strength they be fourscore years,
> yet is their strength labour and sorrow;
> for it is soon cut off, and we fly away.
>
> Psalm 90:10

Epilogue

The major part of this memoir was written in Hong Kong during a very difficult year. Not only was the COVID-19 pandemic sweeping across the globe, but also Hong Kong's pro-democracy movement remained very much uppermost in the minds of many.

Looking back over my lifetime, I realize that I have been blessed with good fortune and never really had to face any of the hardships, suffering or misfortunes which so many people encounter. Unlike my parents and grandparents, I have not been caught up in war, I have never been penniless, and I have not suffered ill health or serious tragedy.

There is no doubt that my 'ten years inside' at Windsor Castle gave me a new perspective on life and was a huge privilege. I was still young in the early years at Windsor but I was able to enjoy life to the full as a teenager in the golden era of the 1960s.

I have never boasted about our time living in the castle. Indeed, I have made it a rule never to raise the subject unless prompted by someone else. But sometimes, during conversation, a friend will let the cat out of the bag and I will be met with an incredulous, questioning look: 'Did you really live *in* the castle?' or 'Did you really meet the Queen?' One of my favourite monikers emanates from this time: Di and I are often known as Prince Philip and Lady Di.

I was also privileged to be head chorister of St George's Chapel, an honour received by few and one of my achievements – even if I was not a devotee of school. I suppose that my love of music, and choral music in particular, stems from this period of my life.

There have been disappointments, of course, usually of my own making. In hindsight, I was probably wrong to leave Marlborough and I was disappointed in my exam results, perhaps due to my lack of application, which put a stop to my reading medicine and going to a more prestigious university.

Readers may have sensed that I have some question marks over my work life. Do not misunderstand me. I have always been deeply interested in the built environment, the interrelationship between people and the buildings in which they live and work. Involvement in the planning, evaluation and development of industrial property and overseas residential complexes has also proved highly rewarding. I have enjoyed my professional career and certainly reaped the benefits of working in Hong Kong, but I am not sure that I ever felt entirely fulfilled in the property business.

Although I was originally destined to be a doctor, this was not to be, and I believe I would have made a good lawyer or academic. Instead, however, I was caught up in the commercial world. Of course, I have always had a great passion for photography, which perhaps I should have pursued – admittedly with the risk of making no money.

I was deeply saddened by the breakdown of my first marriage and headed East in search of a new life. I realized later that it was wrong to 'escape' to Hong Kong when Sarah was just three and a half, a decision which caused me self-reproach, but which I believe was appeased by the close relationship she and I were able to build following her coming to live in Hong Kong in 1994.

Despite my feelings of guilt, heading to Hong Kong proved to be a life-changing experience. It was undoubtedly a high-risk move and I do not believe it advanced my career in the property world. However, it enabled me to take up a second career later in life in photography, publishing and editorial work, which I have found genuinely fulfilling.

But for all the disappointments, there is always a silver lining. The excitement and pace of Hong Kong, exploring a new culture, achieving a lifestyle that Di and I could never have dreamed of in England, having the opportunity to travel extensively, and meeting so many fascinating people from all over the world, many of whom remain close friends to this day: these are the highs.

Setting up my own business, Infocus Media, in 2003 was a milestone for me. It was a very small business – and remains so to this day – but it provided the stimulus to develop my skills in a completely new field and build a good client base. Running the business and still working for one or two clients gives me great satisfaction.

And as I look to the future, I see my daughter, Sarah, Tom and their family flourishing – even in these difficult times. Life continues from generation to generation, each inheriting the experience of our forebears and creating new stories for the next.

In my semi-retirement, I have never once been bored. Di is fully retired and we spend a great deal of time together in our lovely home in Barnes. We both love cooking, we go for walks – albeit not with the vitality of our walks in New Zealand – and we travel when we can, usually enjoying the winter months in Hong Kong.

If you were to ask me what has been the happiest period of my life, I would be hard-pressed to give you an answer. I have enjoyed an enormously satisfying life with a huge amount of fun along the way.

Chronology

- Born in Wells, Somerset, 21st October 1949
- St George's School, Windsor Castle, 1958-63
- Marlborough College, Wiltshire, 1963-66
- Community Service Volunteers, Cardiff, 1967-68
- Brunel University, London – awarded BSc (Hons), 1968-72
- Jones Lang Wootton, Chartered Surveyors, London, 1972-77
- Qualified as an Associate of the Royal Institution of Chartered Surveyors, 1974
- Imperial Foods Ltd, London, 1977-83
- Married Elaine Clare Clay in Ashford, Kent, 6th May 1978
- Sarah Helen Nourse born, 16th September 1980
- Divorced Elaine, 22nd May 1984
- Weatherall, Green & Smith, Chartered Surveyors, London, 1983-84
- Richard Ellis, International Property Consultants, Hong Kong, 1984-85

- Peat Marwick Management Consultants Ltd, Hong Kong, 1985-87
- Touche Ross Management Consultants, London, 1988
- Chesterton Petty Ltd, International Property Consultants, Hong Kong, 1988-2005
- Married Diane Helen Holt in Hong Kong, 8th November 1991
- Mother died in Lympstone, Devon, 23rd May 1992
- Established Infocus Media, 2003
- Bonham Media Ltd, Hong Kong, 2005-2013
- Father died in Exmouth Hospital, Devon, 3rd January 2006
- Sarah and Tom married, 29th July 2016
- Moved to London on a permanent basis, April 2017
- Celebrated threescore years and ten, 21st October 2019